CHAS NEWKEY-BURDEN

ALEXANDRA BURKE

A STAR IS BORN

JOHN BLAKE

Published by John Blake Publishing Ltd
3 Bramber Court, 2 Bramber Road,
London W14 9PB, England

www.johnblakepublishing.co.uk

First published in paperback in 2009

ISBN: 978-1-84454-810-1

British Library Cataloguing-in-Publication Data:

A catalogue record for this book is available from the British Library.

Design by www.envydesign.co.uk

Printed in the UK by CPI Bookmarque, Croydon, CR0 4TD

1 3 5 7 9 10 8 6 4 2

© Text copyright Chas Newkey-Burden 2009

Papers used by John Blake Publishing are natural, recyclable products
made from wood grown in sustainable forests. The manufacturing processes
conform to the environmental regulations of the country of origin.

Photographs © Rex p1, p2, p5, 6, p8; Getty p3; PA p4 and Mirrorpix p7

CONTENTS

FOREWORD

Alexandra Burke burst through the doors leading to the backstage corridor that housed her dressing room at the ITV studios. She was shaking uncontrollably and on the brink of hyperventilation. The 20-year-old North Londoner collapsed against a wall and a tear started running down her cheek. Her shaking and breathing then became even more alarming. She whispered to herself, 'Oh, my God, what's happened to my life?' Falling into the protective arms of fellow contestant Ruth Lorenzo, she burst into hysterical tears.

And this was an hour before the results show crowned her the winner of the fifth series of the smash-hit musical talent show *The X Factor*.

It had been an emotional evening for Alexandra, and one that capped an extraordinary journey. From her childhood in a North London council flat wondering where her father was, through the school years where she endured brutal experiences. Then came the long, hard slog as she chased musical success. While many girls her age would be partying hard, Alexandra had worked hard, *slaved* even, taking every opportunity to sing live, however unglamorous – and some of those opportunities were very unglamorous indeed. This commitment culminated in her first crack at *The X Factor*, which saw her get so near to, yet so far from, success. However, she reacted to that setback as she has all the setbacks in her life: she clenched her fists tighter, held her head high and kept her eyes on the prize, however distant it seemed.

On this evening, the prize was nearly within her grasp. She could almost reach out and touch it. One of three acts in *The X Factor* final, she knew in her heart that this could be her moment. As is customary among contestants, she never publicly admitted to believing she had a chance of victory, and instead insisted her rivals would leave her finishing a distant third. But all week she had been tipped as the favourite, and a smart cookie like Alexandra will have known she was very much in with a chance of winning.

'What's happened to my life?' she had asked herself.

This was after she had performed onstage with her lifelong hero, soul megastar Beyoncé. Onstage, Alexandra sang the first verse and chorus of her idol's hit 'Listen'. The lyrics were perfect for the occasion, as the young hopeful soulfully sang every line about being at a crossroads, and it being the time for her dreams to be heard. It was indeed such a time: the whole nation was sitting up and listening. To be able to sing her hero's song to a live television audience was amazing enough. It was about to get even more amazing for her. 'Ladies and gentlemen, I absolutely cannot believe I am about to introduce this woman to the stage,' she said, as the silhouette of a familiar figure appeared at the back of the stage. 'Please welcome my hero – Beyoncé!'

As Alexandra's emotions simmered to the surface, Beyoncé positively sauntered on to the stage, gave Alexandra a loving, protective look, took her hand and together they duetted the remainder of the song. Despite – or perhaps because of – her emotional state, Alexandra hit all her notes with soulful perfection.

Having nearly broken down with emotion at the song's conclusion, Alexandra staggered to the backstage area as her emotions came simmering to the surface. She eventually composed herself and was ready to sing her final song of the evening, which was her last chance to swing the national vote in her favour. True to form, she sang 'Hallelujah' like a seasoned pro. They talk about performers making songs their own. Well, Alexandra was well and truly claiming ownership of this tune. Then she returned backstage to wait for the results to come through. Once more, she reflected on where she had come from, and where she was going to.

A knock came on her dressing room door. It was time to return to the stage for the results...

INTRODUCTION

Alexandra Burke is living testimony to the power of determination, self-belief and perseverance; her story is an inspiration to all. Although devastated by her rejection from *The X Factor* in 2005, she returned three years later with added zeal and a newfound maturity, and progressed all the way to the final where she was crowned winner. Yet not once throughout her second *X Factor* journey did she make any clichéd defiant statements about proving anyone wrong. Instead, she smiled sweetly, sang even more sweetly and melted the hearts of the viewing public who voted her the winner by a landslide.

'I took three years to get myself ready. I came back

and look what's happened,' she gasped when her victory was confirmed.

But what did happen during those three years? And what is the story of Alexandra's childhood that led to her musical ability and determined nature? Her childhood is full of twists and turns as she shared a cramped bedroom with her sister at night, having performed onstage in front of large crowds. There were tough times for Alexandra as her musical ability and good looks prompted furious envy from school bullies while, at home, her parents' marriage fell apart. Then there was the day when her mother collapsed and was on the brink of death, only to be saved by Alexandra's intervention.

Given all she has gone through, it is little wonder she is such a determined character. She is also a very wise and witty one. Just as her voice entertained us musically throughout her *X Factor* journey, so did her personality shine through. With all due respect to the magnificent Leona Lewis, Alexandra seems to have the edge on her in terms of charisma and personality. There is not just a wit to Alexandra, there is a refreshing, blunt honesty too. When told she was going to sing a cover of 'Hallelujah' as the winner's single, she was the first to say that she was less than impressed with the song choice. She also happily admits that she swore at *X Factor* supreme Simon

Cowell prior to the grand final. 'To get rid of nerves I'd shout, "Fuck it!" just before I went on stage,' she says. 'I even started swearing at Simon Cowell on the phone! We were chatting about the final and I started shouting, "I fucking want this. I fucking want to win!" Luckily, he found it funny and liked the fact I wanted it so badly.'

A source close to Simon Cowell is reported as saying, 'He thinks Alexandra will be a big international star, if they get the music right. In many ways she is more versatile than [Lewis] – she can really dance and there is a greater variety of things that she can do.'

As for Alexandra herself, she would be happy to achieve just a slice of the mammoth success enjoyed by Lewis. 'She is just a girl from Hackney and look what she has done,' says Alexandra, who believes that some of the luck that Hackney girl Lewis enjoyed must have 'taken a bus ride' up to Islington and landed in her lap. She adds, 'I really want to write and sing my own stuff. I hope I have a string of number-one albums and I do make it as an international star. Life experience has meant that I am prepared for the highs and the lows.'

Fortunately for Alexandra, since her X Factor victory, so far she has mostly experienced highs. Her debut single 'Hallelujah' was the Christmas number one and the top-selling album of 2008. She sold 105,000 copies of the single in just 24 hours, becoming the European record holder for single sales. It remained at number one for three weeks – which bodes well for future releases and her career in general. Alexandra's talent and success make her the girl who restored our faith in *The X Factor*. After Leona Lewis had proved what talent can be discovered in reality pop shows, the following year's winner Leon Jackson dampened everyone's enthusiasm after he enjoyed only modest success in the wake of the show. As he flopped, those who look down their disappointed noses at such television programmes had a field day, portraying Lewis as the marvellous exception who proved the rule that *X Factor* victory means only a fleeting moment of fame before anonymity beckons once more.

Then Alexandra came along and wiped the sneers off their faces.

Her voice is sensational and, as Cowell has correctly identified, she has versatility too. As she showed throughout her *X Factor* run, she can perform ballads, up-tempo songs and even big-band classics. During all of these performances, she sang with breathtaking power, worked the required moves with grace and sensuality and – where needed – was always capable of a cheeky smile. Alexandra oozes personality and charisma: quite simply she demands the attention of all who behold her. And that, surely, is what we mean when we talk about 'the x factor'. No wonder she romped home in the final.

No wonder, too, that *X Factor* judge Louis Walsh said, 'Alexandra is going to have a great career in music. Not just in the UK – she can sell records around the world as well.'

Alexandra's mentor Cheryl Cole took her praise and expectations to a different level. 'I hope Alexandra can be as successful as the likes of Leona [Lewis], the likes of Whitney Houston. Just massive, just the biggest it can get. I've got really high hopes for her and really, really a lot of confidence in what she can do.' The next Whitney? High praise indeed.

Rarely has a new artist received such plaudits, and they have not just come from the voting public and the *X Factor* judges. Alexandra has also gained the respect of such musical royalty as Beyoncé, Mariah Carey and Take That, all of whom were particularly impressed with her during their own guest *X Factor* appearances. The rapper 50 Cent, too, has expressed a deep admiration for her and suggested they record a duet one day.

But such praise from music stars is nothing new for Alexandra, who has long been identified as having a special talent by those who know best. Indeed, as a child growing up in North London, her talent was identified by none other than the legendary Stevie Wonder, who wanted her to sign for Motown, but her mother decided it was too early for such a move.

Which brings us to her other 'near miss' – the time that she was sent home in tears from *The X Factor* in 2005 because she had been deemed not ready for the big-time. Louis Walsh was the judge who rejected Alexandra in her first attempt on *The X Factor* and, although he has been mocked by some – including the ever-cheeky Simon Cowell – for his decision in the light of her later triumph, Walsh is correct when he says that he did her a favour back then. Although she sang well on the show, she really wasn't ready to take the world by storm as she was in the 2008 series. In her second attempt, she was transformed, a girl who was peaking at just the right time. She was among the runners-up in the voting patterns until the final three weeks of the competition. Then she took her performances to a new level – not least *that* duet with Beyoncé – and soared into the lead. By the evening of the final, she was in unstoppable, irresistible form. She duly received one million more votes than runners-up JLS.

Upon confirmation of that victory, she was humble and thankful. 'Thank you for making my dreams come true everyone. I have everything to thank you for. In my bones, thank you. I'm the happiest girl. I love you so much.' She was then thrown into the whirlwind of fame and took to it like a natural. Because the truth is that Alexandra is not at all reluctant or awkward about fame – she's a born star, a natural. She is also a positive role model for all. Determined and dignified, she is, in fact, now a star in every sense of the word. To become a star, she has overcome many obstacles. It's been an extraordinary life to date for Alexandra Burke. But let's start at the beginning.

CHAPTER ONE
MUSICAL ROOTS

Alexandra Imelda Cecelia Ewan Burke was born in London on 25 August 1988. 'The Only Way Is Up', Yazz and The Plastic Population's catchy hit, was topping the British charts, and it was a fitting song to welcome the future pop superstar into the world, as the determined, upbeat message contained in the lyrics is one that Alexandra has cleaved to throughout her life. At times she, too, has been broken down, at her lowest turn, but she held on and believed that the only way was up. Her positivity was rewarded – she found brighter days.

The number-one album that week is significant and appropriate too: as compact discs began to outsell vinyl in record stores, Kylie Minogue topped the charts with *Kylie: The Album*. Two decades on, as Alexandra made her bid to become as big a recording artist as Kylie, the Australian superstar's sister Danni was among those who helped her on her way. As for the man who would truly mastermind her rise to prominence, in 1988 Simon Cowell was busy in the recording studio working alongside Pete Waterman, producing hit songs and beginning his majestic journey to the very heights of the music industry. Meanwhile, in the Heaton neighbourhood of Newcastle, five-year-old Cheryl Tweedy was sitting in her tiny bedroom, already dreaming of becoming a performer.

Born under the star sign of Virgo, Alexandra has certainly gone on to display some of the traits associated with that sign. She has buckets of the perfectionism and meticulousness that astrologers say are strong in Virgos, as well as strong Virgo traits of intelligence and wit. But she also noticeably bucks the Virgo trend in several ways. For instance, all who watched her emotional journey on *The X Factor* could hardly call her reserved and undemonstrative. Few would have wanted her to be either: her ardent, outgoing manner was part of her charm as she grew throughout the show and responded with visceral passion and joy at the triumphant conclusion.

Later in her life, weight became an issue for Alexandra when an *X Factor* judge reportedly told her to slim down, although Alexandra insists she only lost weight because she wanted to, not because anyone told her to. All the same, she made a success of it, so much so that the *Mirror* newspaper even used her as an example to other Virgos in their 'Star Sign Diet' feature. 'You're practical and, like fellow Virgo Alexandra Burke, you think things through before making any major decisions. The most health-conscious of all the star signs, improved fitness is likely to be your main motivation for trying to lose weight. Internet dieting is likely to appeal to the more introverted side of your personality.'

Alexandra is a proud Londoner, always describing herself as 'a London girl', and she is a quarter Indian, a quarter Irish, a quarter Jamaican and a quarter English. The district of North London she grew up in reflects this cosmopolitan mix. From the trendy cafes of Upper Street, where middle-class thirty-somethings sit discussing the arts pages of the *Guardian* newspaper and sipping Fair Trade lattes, to the rougher streets of Finsbury Park, it is in many ways a microcosm of the capital city itself. Alexandra grew up on the Caledonian Road, a one-and-half-mile-long road that is known to locals as 'the Cally', which has its own contrasts: the south half of the road is rough and ready, including in its length Pentonville Prison, Ethiopian restaurants and council estates, while the north half is more comfortable. Among those to have been born or raised in Islington are former *X Factor* winner Leona Lewis, pop star Lily Allen and actress Kate Winslet. There are plenty of music venues in Islington and crowds flock to the Scala, Union Chapel and Islington Academy to catch live gigs from a host of artists. Smaller pub venues such as the Hope and Anchor have also developed a cult following among discerning fans of live music.

It was an ideal home environment for Alexandra and her music-loving mother Melissa Bell, a singer of some repute, who found fame in the late 1980s with the sensational music group Soul II Soul. Coincidentally, Bell's route to fame would also begin with a talent contest, albeit a much more low-key affair than the one that catapulted her daughter to stardom 20 years later. She was working as a customer services adviser at the Marble Arch branch of Marks & Spencer, who ran an annual staff karaoke competition. Bell entered the competition and was the runaway winner. Indeed, so powerful and soulful was her performance that her colleagues, seemingly blown away by her previously hidden talents, encouraged her to make a bid for a musical career. Just a week after the karaoke triumph, she handed in her notice. She was on her way to the top, and her next turning on that journey was the highly regarded 291 Talent Show at the famous Hackney Empire in East London, where Bell was about to rock the house.

On hearing that one of the scheduled contestants had dropped out, Bell jumped on to the stage and gave a roof-raising performance of the Gladys Knight classic 'Memories'. It was an astonishing rendition, which earned her a five-minute standing ovation from the appreciative crowd. But, more importantly, after her performance on stage, a representative of Anditone Records approached her and offered her a record deal.

Before long, she had recorded her first single 'Reconsider', and the swinging R&B tune spent almost two months at the number-one spot of the BBC Urban Charts and four weeks at number one of the Kiss FM Sweet Rhythms chart. It was also a regular sound for months on the Choice FM station. All that radio play soon led to radio exposure of a different kind for Bell, who was invited to co-host a BBC Radio One show with Bruno Brookes, where she chatted and sang to the delight of listeners.

The next important call she got was from Soul II Soul front-man Jazzie B, and her place in the band's story beckoned. Whereas soul singers were the predominant influence on Bell, it was a reggae icon that had motivated Jazzie B. 'My dream was to be a DJ and play records at dances in our community. That's the only future I imagined in music because there weren't any black pop stars from Britain. But then Bob Marley came along and it was amazing.

He was one of us and he showed that we could be part of the larger pop world, that we could move beyond our own community – if you worked hard. He kicked down the barriers for most of the black artists who are emerging today.' With such different influences in the Soul II Soul mix, the sound was eclectic and electric.

Having emerged into the musical mainstream in the late-1980s, Soul II Soul won two Grammy awards and had a number of memorable hits including 'Keep On Movin'' and 'Back To Life'. Their look was a huge part of their appeal too: the 'funki dred' tag originating from their dreadlocked front-man Jazzie B. Soul II Soul had ever-changing line-ups and came to be considered as more than just a band. With their 'happy face, thumping bass for a loving race' slogan, they became almost a movement in their own right as their fame became global.

In fact, the relevance of the movement, not just to the music industry but also to the British cultural and political landscape, was immense. Journalist Dotun Adebayo wrote about it in *The Voice* newspaper in 1989, and unwittingly upset Jazzie B in the process. 'I said that Jazzie has a spirit that Margaret Thatcher would be proud of – and he got angry,' he recalls with a smile. 'Jazzie thought I was saying he was a Thatcherite, so he pinned the article on the wall and threw darts at it. But I wasn't talking about politics. I was talking about how he lifted himself up, changing the stereotype of the black musician in Britain and building a whole scene around his music and fashion.'

Political misunderstandings aside, this gives some indication of how significant a band Soul II Soul was.

And for many years Bell was a key part of the band, drawing high praise for her vocals. *The Times*' David Sinclair, in his review of the 1995 album *Volume V Believe*, wrote of 'sterling performances from several other female guest vocalists, notably Melissa Bell on a thoughtful ballad called "Be a Man"'.

Since her days with Soul II Soul, Bell has toured the world, singing alongside such musical royalty as George Michael, Liza Minnelli, Queen, The Who, Elton John and Stevie Wonder.

So it is hardly surprising that such musical talent rubbed off on the young Alexandra, whose love of music and ability for singing emerged early on. There was always music playing in the household and Bell is clear who the biggest musical influence on her daughter was. 'I was!' she declares proudly.

Alex agrees, citing her mother alongside the other musicians who influenced her as a child, both in the introductions she offered and in her own right. 'Mum introduced me to some of the greatest singers – Gladys Knight, Al Green, Whitney, Mariah, Aretha – and whenever she was on tour I'd always be listening to them – and her.'

At the age of five, Alexandra used to stroll around the Islington housing-association maisonette where they lived, singing soul classics, and so it seems her neighbours were the first people to – indirectly – attend an Alexandra Burke concert. Bell recalls her daughter's early musicianship vividly. 'Alex has been singing since she was five. She grew up listening to me, copying me and following my advice – I just hope she goes further than I did.'

But, of course, Bell's primary influence on Alexandra was as a parent, rather than a musical mentor, and it was quite a struggle for her to raise not just Alexandra, but also her other three children: Sheneice, who is two years older than Alexandra; David Jr, who is one year older; and Aaron who is four years her junior. That task became even more difficult when she split from her husband David, who she had married at the age of 20, when Alexandra was just 6 years old.

As a child, Alexandra would often ask her mother where Daddy was and Melissa would have to make up excuses, even though David lived just five miles away in central London. It was a tough time for the whole family. 'We were left to struggle, my mum, me, my two brothers and my sister, Sheneice,' remembers Alexandra. 'She and I shared a bed for years, which wasn't very comfortable. But singing kept me going.' These were testing times for Alexandra, as she was forced to try to reconcile loyalty to her mother with the fact that she missed her father. 'He was in and out of our lives,' she says. 'I hardly saw him growing up. He would call up one day then we wouldn't hear from him for months. Even when he was away we loved him dearly. Understandably, Mum wants nothing to do with him.'

These were also difficult times for Alexandra's mother, who was battling diabetes. Bell's own mother, Ivy, had died of diabetes-related complications in 1992 but, when she was diagnosed with diabetes herself, she says she buried her head in the sand. After the birth of Sheneice, Bell had first noticed something was wrong. 'I was tired all the time and constantly thirsty, which at first I put down to the pregnancy,' she says. After several months, though, she felt so unwell that she went to a GP for a test. 'I was devastated when the GP confirmed it was type-two diabetes,' Bell told the *Daily Mail*. 'I remember saying that I didn't want to die. He reassured me, saying my condition could be monitored and controlled.' All the same, she says, she did not heed the warnings that both the medical profession and her late mother had offered. 'Mum warned me about the dangers of diabetes but I didn't listen,' she says with a sigh. 'And just the thought I couldn't eat cakes and biscuits made me want them more. I could not stick to a diet that would have helped me manage my diabetes.' The combination of her mother's death and her own medical condition sent Bell into despair, which she tried to hide from her family. 'Every morning I would wake up, almost surprised to still be there. It was a very dark time. Like all my children, Alex was very supportive but she was still young. They weren't aware of how bad I was feeling.'

With her mother battling illness and often touring the world with Soul II Soul in order to earn enough money to keep the family afloat, Alexandra and her siblings were left in the care of their grandfather Ivan and a childminder named Pauline Harty, who Alexandra refers to as her 'second mother'. Her mother's travelling meant that she missed nearly all of Alexandra's performances, including school plays and performances. It was naturally upsetting for the youngster as she looked into an audience filled with expectant, proud parents, not to see either her mother or father there. A combination of focus and understanding saw her through. 'You know what? I've always had the drive to do it regardless. Don't get me wrong, it did upset me, but I knew she was always busy, always providing.' However, since making this conciliatory remark, Alexandra has been more direct about how hurt she has been by her mother's absence. 'Every birthday my mum would send me £50 in the post. She was away on tour a lot,' she remembers. 'She was making money for us and living her dream but all I wanted was for her to be around more. The one thing I hated was when she was away. I can say now, it's a shame that my mum never came to a school performance because she was always away. That's the one thing I really kicked her for. It was my granddad who was at them all. My granddad and my auntie Sonia were there for me all the time.' She has also admitted how upset she was that her mother did not attend the first week of the live finals of *The X Factor* in 2008.

Her mother's absence during her childhood is clearly still a difficult issue for Alexandra, who has given as many understanding, conciliatory statements about the subject as she has more critical ones. It is not surprising that the loving and loyal Alexandra should feel mixed up, and perhaps she will always feel conflicted on this matter. 'I owe my life to them, they're a very supportive family,' she says when asked about her close relatives. 'Every family has their ups and downs, and I thank God that we now are a secure family. We are a tight family and my mum is like my best mate, my sister as well, it's ridiculous.'

But, despite her mixed feelings about her mum's career, it provided an opportunity for Alexandra's first significant stage appearance. 'One day, when she was nine, I was doing a corporate gig in front of four hundred people and Alex got up out of the audience, walked up to the stage and said, "Mum, can I sing?"'

remembers Melissa. 'She took the mic and sang "Coco Jumbo", a popular dance song, and the audience loved it. She had a kind of mesmerising star quality, even then.'

In fact, 'Coco Jumbo' is a rather masculine and mature song for a nine-year-old girl to sing. Performed by the three-piece German Europop act Mr President, it is a catchy reggae-fused tune that gave the band their biggest hit. With its lyrics about taking a 'pee pee' and 'treating girls smooth', it must have seemed an extraordinary performance from such a young child. However, the truly extraordinary aspect was the sheer quality of her vocal performance. As Bell gushes, 'That was the first time I thought, Wow, she could really make a go of this. After that, she took every opportunity to come to the recording studios and she did backing vocals on many of my tracks.'

The same year, Alexandra had another live-performance experience courtesy of her talented and loving mother. Bell had been called to perform in Bahrain, and had brought Alexandra with her. During one of the performances, she handed a microphone to her daughter and told her to sing to the audience. It was a defining moment for Alexandra. 'I knew I wanted to sing from the age of five, but that was the first time I got that kick,' she says. She sang the Randy Crawford number 'You Might Need Somebody' and absolutely mesmerised the audience. 'I love that song,' she says. Three years later she would sing it to a much larger audience.

At this point, Alexandra was coming to the end of her primary-school education, at the mixed Copenhagen Primary School, which is a mere stone's throw from the Regents Canal in North London. For her secondary education, she moved to the Elizabeth Garrett Anderson School, an all-girl comprehensive in Barnsbury, where she was required to wear a uniform. To get to school in the mornings, she would walk through the nearby lively Chapel Street Market, with its stalls hawking everything from fruit and fish to household goods and clothes, and its traditional pie-and-mash outlet. The school prides itself on being strict on punctuality and attendance, and it also boasts that it nurtures pupils to the very highest levels of achievements, with its slogan of 'learning without limits'. Very quickly, the staff there became aware of Alexandra's very obvious musical talent.

The head of music at the school, Sarah Beagley, was proud of the reputation the establishment had for its musical output and she was one of the first to notice how richly Alexandra's singing voice was developing. Appropriately enough, given Alexandra's later route to fame, the setting was a talent contest. 'I will never forget the first time I heard Alexandra sing before an audience,' recalls Beagley. 'She was just eleven and she entered our talent competition and was up against twenty-four other girls, some of them sixteen years old. As she opened her mouth to sing "You Might Need Somebody" by Shola Ama, a chill went up my spine. She had such a powerful voice and such a deep, resonant sound that I looked at my fellow judges and I could tell we were all thinking the same thing: she's only eleven! She blew us away. When she finished, the pupils rose to their feet and gave her a thunderous ovation.' It was like a moment from a feel-good teen movie and the triumph turned out to be complete. 'She won, which was some achievement given that we were a school renowned for its performing arts,' Beagley says, smiling.

Alexandra had blown away the audience and her teacher. Over the coming five years, Beagley would work to polish Alexandra's talent so she could reach her highest potential. With the help of voice coach Alison Campbell, she turned Alexandra's raw talent into genius. You could say she put a bit of extra 'x factor' into the mix – and much more besides. 'We taught her keyboard skills, how to read music, how to broaden her range and, most importantly, we developed her breathing technique so she could sing technically correctly and not damage her vocal cords,' remembers Beagley. 'She was a model student: always on time, well prepared, and incredibly self-assured in a modest way. She had a three-octave range, which is pretty handy, and in the school choir she could sing low alto to top soprano.'

Later in life, Alexandra would receive praise from *The X Factor* judges but none of them would be quite so musically technical.

It was a fine school choir and Alexandra fitted in perfectly. Her timing was ideal, as at this time the school choir was approached by a very prestigious talent, Jamaican-born Sir Willard White, a bass-baritone opera singer who was knighted in 2004 for his services to music. So you can imagine the excitement that went through the school when the choir was approached to provide backing singers for Sir Willard for his performance of the oratorio *El Nino* at London's prestigious Barbican Theatre. During the rehearsals, Sir Willard approached Beagley and asked, 'Who's that girl with the big voice? She's going to be a star.' How right he has proved to be.

Beagley is enormously proud of her part in Alexandra's story, and rightly so. But she also acknowledges that Bell was Alexandra's true mentor. 'Although we still keep in touch and I am immensely proud of her, it's her mum who has been her most profound influence. Having said that, the driving force in Alex's life has always been Alex herself. By the time she left school at sixteen after completing her GCSEs, she'd gone from a little girl with a big voice to somebody with star quality.'

However, that star quality came with a price for young Alexandra. She was bullied by jealous classmates who threw cruel taunts at the emerging star and pulled her hair, and she would often come home in tears. In fact, she admits that as a result of all this she has self-confidence issues to this day. One of the criticisms that has been thrown at *The X Factor* is that many of the contestants seem to bring 'sob stories' to the show and rely on pulling the audience's heartstrings for votes. As we shall see, Alexandra rose above such temptation and bravely eschewed numerous opportunities to go down the 'pity route', and instead let her talent speak – or rather sing – for itself. But she has encouraged bullied youngsters to believe in themselves. She says of her experience of bullying, 'It improved as the years went on,' and she advises today's victims, 'Don't give up. You have something strong inside you.'

Alexandra too had something strong inside her and was about to prove it in style.

CHAPTER TWO

STAR FOR A NIGHT

*T*he *X Factor* was not the first television talent
show Alexandra had entered, as nearly a decade
earlier she had appeared on *Star For A Night*. She
recalls, 'I entered when I was twelve [which made her
the youngest person in the competition] on BBC1.
I didn't win the show though!'

Star For A Night was hosted by singer, actress
and television presenter Jane McDonald, who was
discovered on the BBC1 docu-soap *The Cruise* and
became a star overnight. The show's 14 million
viewers loved her. One of her first jobs after *The
Cruise* was fronting *Star For A Night*; the format
was simple and winning, and the lady from Yorkshire
was perfect. McDonald would surprise people during
their everyday lives, telling them they had been
nominated to appear and sing on the show. The lucky

people would then have a week auditioning and rehearsing before singing in front of the nation and a judging panel, who would ultimately decide who had won the show.

Alexandra's performance on it was memorable, giving an early hint of how emotional and amusing she could be, and also how comfortable she was with speaking and singing on television. Her shock as McDonald approaches her in the classroom will be familiar to those who saw her similar reaction when she won *The X Factor*. She is practising at the school keyboard when she looks up and notices McDonald and the camera crew. 'Oh, my God!' she squeals and holds her hands to her mouth in shock.

'Alex, congratulations,' says McDonald, 'you're on *Star For A Night*!'

In her subsequent interview on the show, a more composed Alexandra admitted, 'It was quite a big surprise, what they did, 'cause I never knew I'd be so emotional like that.' Wearing a sleeveless leopard-print top and already completely at home in the television-interview environment, she spoke with a sweet, witty innocence. Turning to the audition she had to give at the beginning of the week, she said, 'I felt scared because I thought, They're not going to want me in. I had too much make-up on my face, my hair was all out everywhere and I was wearing trousers that kept falling off. I had

to keep pulling them up. I'm not wearing them
again.'

Footage of her wearing the pink trousers in
question shows that she looked great, and this was
perhaps childish self-consciousness at work behind
her concern over her appearance.

Next up for Alexandra during her dream week
came the rehearsals, which took her to a new level of
performance and gave her a whole new experience. 'In
the rehearsal, I've never actually been with a
choreographer that helps you with dance moves,' she
said, smiling. 'I've only just made them up myself. It's
actually quite fun because I'm dancing with really
great people behind me. They can dance really well.'
Meanwhile, she was featured during the rehearsals,
wearing a blue and white top and working hard on
her dance moves. Asked how she would feel when she
finally stood up on stage to perform on television, her
excitement was palpable. 'I'm going to feel hyper
because when I'm nervous I start to shiver and then
once I let my energy out I'll start to relax. Then I'll be
able to perform.' She added, 'When I get older, yes, I
do want to be a singer. I'm fortunate to be here
tonight. The song that I'm singing I want to dedicate
it to my mum. So, Mum, this one's for you!'

As Alexandra stood nervously backstage, she was
led to the wings and told she would be on stage any
minute. Her nerves built up, just as she had predicted,

but performance-wise it was all right on the night for Alexandra. In front of a live studio audience and millions of viewers, a beaming Jane McDonald said, 'From North London, here's Alexandra Burke!'

With a deep breath, Alexandra stepped out on to the stage. Wearing a white sleeveless top and white trousers, she looked a million dollars. As the backing track kicked in, she showed she could dance as well as sing, making full use of the stage and pulling off some great hand movements as part of her performance. Young Alexandra launched into the first verse of the song, with its lyrics of 'opening up your heart and letting friends in'. Midway through the verse, she was joined by the group of dancers. Between them they put in a cracking performance, which had the audience – including schoolfriends of Alexandra – in raptures. As the song came to an end, Alexandra gave the camera a winning smile and then bowed graciously. She was indeed a star for the night.

However, she was not to be the winner that night. Instead, a 12-year-old from Devon called Joss Stone came out on top over Alexandra and the boy who had impersonated Robbie Williams. The judging panel, which included Jane McDonald, actress Barbara Windsor and actress Natalie Cassidy, Sonia from *EastEnders*, deemed Stone's version of the Donna Summer song 'On The Radio' the best on the night. Looking back on her part in the show, the now world-famous Stone says she isn't sure why she even entered. 'Don't ask me, man. I was twelve. I dunno. There were, like, two seconds of my life when I thought, OK, I'm going to do it. And I did.' As a result of her triumph that night, she was approached by a series of managers and music producers wanting to represent her. She has since released multi-platinum-selling albums and received a nomination for a Grammy.

Although Alexandra lost out to Stone on the night, there were no hard feelings. Indeed, the pair hit it off and quickly became friends, and their lives and careers have continued to intertwine ever since.

Further excitement was to come for Alexandra that year in the form of a phone call to the family home. Even given the musical royalty that made up much of her mother's address book, young Alexandra could never have guessed who was on the phone when she strolled up and lifted the receiver. Indeed, even once she found out who it was, she didn't quite believe it. After all, it is not every day that Stevie Wonder phones up. 'I was really cheeky,' remembers Alexandra. 'I was twelve and didn't believe it was him! I said, "If you are Stevie Wonder, sing to me." He sang "Isn't She Lovely" – there was no doubt it was him.'

You can only imagine her horror and embarrassment when she realised she had doubted the legendary Stevie Wonder. Red-faced, toes curling and trembling, she stumbled over her apology.

Luckily, Wonder showed as much class on the phone as he does on the stage. 'He insisted we had a three-way call with my mum,' says Alexandra. 'Then he asked to hear one of my demos.'

For Alexandra, holding a conversation on the phone with Stevie Wonder must have been amazing enough. But to then be asked by him to play some of her music down the phone was surely mind blowing. She quickly hit 'play' and let Wonder hear her beautiful young singing voice. Wonder enthused about what he heard and told Alexandra and her mother that he wanted to sign her to the legendary Motown label. However, it was not to be. 'Mum said I was too young,' Alexandra says with a shrug. Still, Stevie Wonder had called and said he loved her talent, which was an enormous boost to her self-confidence as her musical talent developed. (Wonder was also very fulsome in his praise for Bell, saying in 2002, 'This lady has a world-class voice'.) The following year, Alexandra met Wonder – quite by chance – in a London venue and the legend has kept in touch with her ever since. Quite a name to have in your little black book as a teenager!

This was just one brush with a famous artist that young Alexandra enjoyed. One day, Bell took advantage of her friendship with American jazz and soul singer Jean Carne by asking her to listen to Alexandra sing. The highly regarded Carne, who has recorded alongside other stars and in her own right since the 1960s, was mightily impressed with this fledgling talent and demanded that Alexandra perform on stage with her the following night. Naturally, Alexandra needed little persuasion!

But, as well as actually meeting stars, Alexandra also dreamed of them. Indeed, she was a real dreamer during her childhood, often sitting in her bedroom imagining becoming a singing star. She also watched *Top Of The Pops* intently and, while glued to the screen, she dreamed of her own idols who inspired, influenced and enlivened her. Chief among these was Beyoncé, who first caught Alexandra's attention as the lead singer of girl group Destiny's Child before going on to become a global solo megastar. 'I love Beyoncé so much, oh, my God, it's a joke!' she says. If I could only be like her, thought young Alexandra. She also dreamed of meeting her idols, and her dreams would come true as her talent and hard work were rewarded handsomely later in her life.

It is worthwhile pausing to reflect just how far Alexandra had already come by the age of 12. At the same age, Leona Lewis – who won the 2007 *X Factor* – had written her first song and her parents were struggling to get the money together to put her through the Sylvia Young Theatre School, and to build a recording studio for her in their home. However, by this age, Alexandra had sung to large live audiences in two different continents of the world, appeared on a high-ratings television show and had wowed the great Jean Carne so much with her voice that she was invited to sing on stage with her. She had also played a demo of her material down the phone to none other than Stevie Wonder, who was blown away by her talent. Her first 12 years had indeed been remarkable times for Alexandra.

But the best was yet to come; the girl with the angelic voice from an Islington council estate was ready to take more steps up the ladder to fame, fortune and recognition. Soon, those cruel taunts from the school bullies would be a distant memory and nothing was going to hold this girl back because an exciting new trend was developing in the world of television broadcasting that would change Alexandra's life for ever.

CHAPTER THREE

X MARKS
THE SPOT

As the 12-year-old Alexandra was being bullied in school, television bosses were putting the finishing touches to the first show in a new genre that would ultimately put her head and shoulders above all who had taunted her. ITV's *Popstars* was going to take the talent-show concept firmly into the 21st century. During a six-week period late in 2000, thousands of young hopefuls auditioned in front of three judges – and ITV viewers – who then narrowed down the field to five people who formed a band called Hear'say. However, that brief synopsis doesn't begin to do justice to the sea of change that *Popstars* brought to British broadcasting – a change that was ultimately to transform Alexandra's life. The public loved watching the now familiar format of drama and heartbreak that *Popstars* brought to our screens. The head of the judging panel, Nigel Lythgoe, was quickly dubbed 'Nasty Nigel' due to the directness of his comments. Lythgoe was a television legend, having commissioned and produced shows including *Gladiators* and *Blind Date*, but it would be *Popstars* that would leave the biggest legacy, not just in British broadcasting but also around the world. And as the series was broadcast, one viewer watched with a mixture of admiration and disappointment.

Record-label executive Simon Cowell had been approached to be a part of the judging panel for *Popstars* but had turned down the offer, uneasy at the idea of television showing the world the process of putting a band together. Cowell thought this should be kept mysterious, believing that showing such a process on television for all to see was akin to a magician explaining how he does his tricks. Then, as he sat watching the resultant show go out, he realised he'd made a huge mistake. The show was a massive success and made for brilliant television. He kicked himself for turning down the chance to take part and then picked up the phone to Simon Fuller. Within a matter of months, they had finalised the details of a new show that would take the *Popstars* concept to a whole new level. Television, and the music industry, would never be the same again.

Pop Idol was a smash-hit show. It combined the

success of the *Popstars* format with a crucial new ingredient – the public vote. Channel 4's *Big Brother* show had proved that when the public are given the chance to vote on the outcome of a show it makes for a far more dramatic and engrossing experience. Viewers care more when they get a say in the outcome, which means better viewing figures and the colossal revenue stream that can be raised by the phone-in votes. Cowell and Fuller knew they had a hit on their hands but even they might have been taken aback by just how well *Pop Idol* did. It began broadcasting in the autumn of 2001 and the initial stages were familiar to anyone who had watched *Popstars*: hopefuls auditioning in front of a panel and being put through or dismissed. At this stage of the competition, the judges had the sole say in who went through and who did not. And what a say it was, particularly in the case of Cowell who took the 'nasty' position on the panel. He surpassed any nastiness that Lythgoe had managed and offered put-downs that shocked and engrossed the nation. As with *Popstars*, the combination of the brilliant, the average and the downright terrible contestant field made for must-see television.

Once the final 50 contestants were agreed on by the judges, the audience voting came into effect. The judges still gave their verdicts each week – something Cowell had insisted on, against initial plans to remove the judges from the show at this stage – but the public decided who went home and who stayed in. Eventually, the field was reduced to a final ten and at this point proceedings moved to a live Saturday final in front of a studio audience. By this time the show became little short of a national obsession. One contestant, Berkshire boy Will Young, had answered back to Cowell's criticisms and as such become a favourite to win. Another favourite was Gareth Gates, a Yorkshire boy who had a stutter when he spoke but the voice of a choir boy when he sang.

Those two contestants were to be the last men standing and they battled it out in an epic final. All week they had toured the UK in separate 'campaign buses' emblazoned with their faces. The nation was going *Pop Idol* crazy and everyone in the country, it almost seemed, had a favourite of the two. The final itself was watched by over 12 million viewers. On the night, posh Young edged the voting and beat cherubic Gates to become the first Pop Idol, winning a record contract, and he went on to become a top-selling pop artist.

Young recalled that when he was told by how many votes the winner had one – prior to the actual outcome being revealed – he assumed he had come second. 'I thought, I am second and I have lost by that much. I promise, I just thought, Oh well, that's not bad,' he said with a smile. 'And then they said it and

I just, I don't know, I felt really isolated. I stepped backwards. I could not believe it.' Speaking backstage after the show, he said, 'I am really ready for it now. I am just up for it massively, in a huge way.'

And it seemed the nation was up for reality television in a huge way. In fact, it had been quite a night not just for television and the music industry, nor even just for Young the winner, but for the entire nation. A BT spokesperson said the volume of calls to the show as viewers feverishly voted for their favourite act had threatened the national network, and the company was forced to limit the number of calls that got through. Meanwhile, the National Grid called ITV to check commercial-break times amid genuine fears of a power cut from huge surges in electricity demands. This was more than a television show, it had become something of a national phenomenon more akin to a general election. And, while Young might have triumphed in the voting, the real winners were the two Simons: Cowell and Fuller, who had created a monstrously successful television show. Plans were immediately made for a second series; if the success of the first series could be replicated the next time round, ITV might just have a new television institution on their hands.

However, the second series – despite all the viewers' anticipation – turned out to be a major disappointment. True, the early stages proved entertaining as a combination of the weird, wonderful and woeful lined up to audition in front of the judges. But, even at this stage, something didn't seem quite right. The savvy contestants were now aware of how the show worked and this time they came expecting harsh, withering comments from Cowell, and they were often ready with suitable retorts. With the element of shock removed from the equation, much of the spontaneity and appeal appeared to have been taken away for the viewer. More importantly, there was a definite shortage of talent and characters. In series one, there had been plenty of both but this time round the contestants seemed less engrossing.

Accordingly, Cowell took to championing Scot singer Michelle McManus, a large young lady who spoke of her determination to not let size issues prevent her from making it big. 'I want to break the mould of pop,' she said. Cruel Internet wags suggested that perhaps she should just sit on it. Judge Pete Waterman was also dismissive of her and insistent that she should not become the Pop Idol. However, her case is instructive to this story, as indirectly she can be seen to have led to the creation of *The X Factor*, which catapulted Alexandra to the top of the charts and stardom.

It is a mark of the influence of *Pop Idol* that the controversy over McManus reached the heights of the

House of Commons. There, MP Jim Sheridan tabled an early day motion, signed by nine others, that urged the show to stop focusing on McManus's physique. It said, 'That this House condemns the irresponsible comments of the so-called music experts on this programme when passing their judgements on the young performers. Pressurising young people, and women in particular, to conform to fit the mould sends out the wrong message, not only to the participants but to the other talented youngsters who may also have aspirations to progress in the music industry.' The motion added that contestants should be judged solely on 'their unique singing talents and not on preconceived images'.

Pop Idol producer Claire Horton defended her show and the way it went about its work with McManus and all the contestants. She said, '*Pop Idol* gave Kim and Michelle the opportunity to get into the music industry despite them not having the stereotypical look of a pop star. If the judges were concerned about image they would not have put them through to the final fifty and the audience would not have voted them through to what is now the final eight. I am honoured, however, that the programme is so important that it is being discussed in the House of Commons.'

It was indeed an honour, and a reflection of the growing stature and influence of the reality pop genre.

Soon the BBC were getting in on the act with *Fame Academy*, their own take on the format.

As for McManus, the lady who prompted the House of Commons motion, she defended herself and seemed very comfortable. 'I feel good about myself and I never get upset with my size,' she said. 'I have no intention of losing any more weight. It's not that I don't care about myself but I'm happy the way I am. I think it is positive that people are voting for me because of my size. Although all women pop stars look good, people want something different, something to represent them.' That said, the Scot was quite understandably less than pleased with comparisons that had been made between her and rock star Meat Loaf. She said, 'I don't think I look like Meat Loaf. He is not attractive. I think I'm attractive. I'm not the most stunning woman but I'm not ugly.'

Cowell continued to back and praise her to the hilt and she made it all the way to the final, where she competed with affable Brummie Mark Rhodes. But this final line-up had none of the charm and intensity of the Young/Gates rivalry of the series-one final. On the night, Cowell continued to praise McManus wildly, almost appearing to be her mentor at times – an aspect that would have ramifications for his next television project. 'You know at the end of the day you've got a load of votes, you deserve to be here,' he told her. 'I think if you weren't in the final it would have been quite boring. Hey, it would have been because, you know, you've broken the norm, you know, you've made it interesting, I'm interested. And I'm very proud that you're here, Michelle, I really am. And good for you.'

In the end, McManus won but little could hide the disappointment many felt over every aspect of the second series. Waterman's storm-out from the studio might have been dramatic but it reflected the feelings of many that the second series had come nowhere near to replicating the magic of series one. The *Daily Telegraph*, for instance, summed up the final rather acidly as a competition between 'Mama Cass and a Butlins Red Coat'. Waterman was more succinct, claiming the programme had become 'a freak show'.

But, regardless of the criticism of the quality of the second series, McManus was naturally overjoyed at winning the competition. 'Whether it lasts a year or twenty years, I'm going to give it my best shot,' she said when asked about her victory. 'I just want to do really well and I'll break my back in trying. I haven't come from anywhere – I was nobody six months ago. I am part of the British public and we won't vote for people because we feel sorry for them, we vote for them because they are talented.'

Once more, politics blended with pop as Scottish First Minister Jack McConnell said he voted for McManus and congratulated her on winning *Pop*

Idol. 'Michelle brought sparkle to the contest and real hope and then pride to Scotland,' he said. 'This is a big signal to young Scots, if you have the ambition and go for it, you can win.'

Then in a statement that foreshadowed a similar announcement from Alexandra on her *X Factor* victory five years later, winner McManus declared that she was not going to be dating in the aftermath of her victory. 'I've always had boyfriends and this is the first time I have been really *Bridget Jones* single, and I'm loving it,' said the Scot. 'I've got no time for men.'

But, sadly, the music industry proved to have little time for McManus. She had been widely expected to flop, including by Westlife manager – and future reality pop show judge, who would have an enormous bearing on Alexandra's career – Louis Walsh. The Irishman predicted, 'I don't think she's going to do well. I think she's like the new Jane McDonald, just a larger version. She'll be good for cruise ships – big cruise ships. I don't know why she won but she did, and we have to give her her fifteen minutes, but I don't see a long career.'

She had a number-one single and number-three album in the immediate aftermath of the show but since then McManus had become better known for her celebrity dieting ventures than for her singing. McManus's case is highly relevant to the Alexandra story. She represented the flop that *Pop Idol* took in series two and that flop led to the development of *The X Factor*, through which Alexandra would ultimately find fame and fortune.

However, it would be unfair and misleading to suggest that McManus was responsible for the downturn in the fortunes of the *Pop Idol* show. It had been a bad year for the whole show second time round and there were doubts as to whether the format had already exhausted itself. Perhaps, it was argued, there were just not enough good young acts in Britain to keep swelling the numbers in reality pop shows. Maybe *Pop Idol* should have stayed as a marvellous one-off success, after which reality television and pop should be kept separate?

But Simon Cowell certainly did not subscribe to this belief. In 2004, he unveiled a brand-new reality pop show, which would be a joint venture between his Syco company and the record label BMG. It would be called *The X Factor* and it would revolutionise Saturday-night television.

One of the key differences between *Pop Idol* and *The X Factor* was that the new show would allow bands to audition and would also open its doors to older contestants than had been allowed on *Pop Idol*. The other main change was that *The X Factor* would see each of the judges mentor a category instead of merely sitting behind a desk and offering criticisms.

They would have to walk it like they talked it and try to guide their own acts to victory. As Tim Bowen, BMG UK and Ireland chairman, said at the launch, 'I am delighted. Simon and his team have really hit the ground running with this new show. The judges have become the contestants and now we will see how creative they really are.'

Cowell, too, was delighted to be linking up with BMG for the series. Not that he had lacked other offers. 'Of course, the money is nice,' he said of his decision to go with BMG. But it was more than that, he said. 'Look, it's very easy for a lot of companies to go, "We would love you to come and do the same thing for us." But when I was on the open market, probably about 17 or 18 years ago, there was only one company who were prepared to back me and that was BMG. That support has been there for eighteen years. It's easy to say, when you are successful, "I will go and do this elsewhere." But I felt, particularly when we did this last negotiation, that there was still this debt from me to them I had to pay off, which was "You put me in this position – you helped me do this, so I still owe you something."'

Explaining his decision to introduce the mentor element into the show, Cowell explained that he was trying 'to put a sense of ownership and responsibility on the judges'. Of his decision to open up the field to older contestants, he explained that he was 'bored with just watching twenty-two- or twenty-three-year-olds coming on to a talent show and saying, "Make me famous". It's more interesting opening it up to everyone so you can tell more stories.'

Joining him on the panel would be Sharon Osbourne, music manager and wife of Ozzy, who was no stranger to reality television, having been the hilarious matriarch of *The Osbournes* show. She was also no stranger to Cowell. 'I'd met him once before and interviewed him on my American chat show,' she said. 'He'd struck me as a pompous, spoiled little boy. But doing *The X Factor* was a good decision. Two of my children – Aimee and Jack – were thinking of moving back to the UK, which meant we could all live in our house in Buckinghamshire.'

The other judge joining Cowell on the panel was Irishman Louis Walsh, who had managed Boyzone and Westlife. The three judges were to have a far more cantankerous relationship than that enjoyed between judges on previous shows. Cowell actively encouraged banter and rivalry between them. On *The X Factor*, more than on similar shows, one almost felt at times that the judges were the true stars of the show. 'Nasty' Nigel Lythgoe, whose attitude Cowell seemed to adapt and extent, was impressed by *The X Factor*-era Cowell. He said, 'Simon's really got his act together now. When he started out, he wasn't very quick witted and he didn't have a sense of humour, he was just nasty. But he's grown tremendously and he hasn't simply moved into the part, he *is* the part now.'

Meanwhile, Osbourne took a more motherly approach to her verdicts, though she could be bitchy too at times, and Walsh floated between being prickly and cuddly.

The presence of older contestants immediately gave *The X Factor* a whole new dynamic compared with *Pop Idol*, with Cowell hopeful that a more mature act could prove a huge success for the show. 'I would like someone who sells as many records as Cliff [Richard],' he said. 'We have seen some real talent in the older age group. Somebody aged 50 could easily win this competition.' However, he did feel there was a limit. 'Louis and Sharon have sent through 81-year-olds. One woman was very sweet but she was just too old. She couldn't get up the stairs without three people giving her a hand.'

Cowell admitted that, although reality pop shows around the world had been a huge on-screen success, it was yet to be regularly matched off screen in terms of the success of the artists spawned by the programmes. 'Yeah, I do go along with that, to an extent,' he said. 'From the US and the UK combined, if we are being honest, we have one international artist so far, which is Kelly Clarkson, someone who has gone on to sell all over the world. It's a good thing and a bad thing. It's a bad thing that we haven't got more but the good thing is that, if she can do it, if we can find someone like that from the show, there's no reason we can't do that again.'

Indeed, he was very hopeful that his new series *The X Factor* would be the one that struck gold. 'You have to be optimistic and hope and believe that one year you are going to find someone who can become a true multi-platinum international artist. But there's no guarantee. You just have a better chance with this show than you normally do when you sign an artist.'

Ironically, *The X Factor* would follow an opposite trend to that of *Pop Idol*. It would get greater artists later in its run, rather than peaking early and then dropping off. Before that, though, Cowell found himself facing a lawsuit from Simon Fuller, the man he had with worked on *Pop Idol*, which led to fears that the entire *X Factor* bandwagon might collapse. After watching the opening show of the series, Fuller said he noted 25 similarities between *The X Factor* and *Pop Idol*, including everything from the stage set-up, music, logos and lighting to the way the judges were seated and contestants lined up for the auditions. Fuller's company 19 TV, which created *Pop Idol* and *American Idol*, launched legal action against producer FremantleMedia, Cowell and his firms Simco and Syco. A 19 spokesman said that '19 TV will be pressing for a speedy trial to resolve the matters as swiftly as is possible'.

FremantleMedia – whose Talkback Thames subsidiary produces *X Factor* – said in a statement, 'We deny the allegations made in the writ and in the press. We will defend any action vigorously and we hope to resolve the matter amicably.' It added, '*The X Factor* is a different format to *Pop Idol*.'

Cowell branded it 'utterly ridiculous', while his spokesman, legendary PR guru Max Clifford, told the BBC, 'Does this mean that Granada could sue the BBC for creating *EastEnders* because it made *Coronation Street* first? Look at New *Faces*, *Opportunity Knocks*, there have always been television talent programmes.'

Finally, in November 2005, as Alexandra battled her way through the second series of *The X Factor*, the pair settled out of court. 'We're delighted with the outcome. People think we hate each other but we don't. We're good friends,' Cowell said, and later added, 'Even throughout the last lawsuit, which probably lasted 18 months, we must have had dinner on five or six occasions. I knew why he had issued us with the lawsuit and I think he knew why I had launched *X Factor*. There was a kind of understanding that only he and I understood really and, because we understand both positions, it didn't feel particularly personal. I never thought it was going to go to court, so I treated the whole thing as kind of like paperwork.'

But, while the case had rumbled on behind the scenes, the first series of *The X Factor* had hit TV screens and had been a roaring success. Alexandra watched the show from her North London home and, the more the series went on, the more she thought that here was a great chance for her to make her ambitions reality. The final three in the series were middle-aged crooner Steve Brookstein, Irish rocker Tabby Callaghan and opera boy band G4. The semi-final saw Callaghan voted off, leaving a straight fight between G4 (mentored by Walsh) and Brookstein (mentored by Cowell). It proved to be a dramatic final.

After Brookstein sang his final song of the night – 'Against All Odds' by Phil Collins – he was turned on by an irate Osbourne. 'Listen, everybody knows the way I feel about Steve. I've never been a Steve fan,' she said. 'Steve has a very nice voice. For me he's not a superstar. And I just have to say this... I am so fed up of Mr Humble and Mr "Should I sell my Volkswagen? Should I keep it?" He's over confident, he's been over confident from day one! He is... he's not what he seems, believe me! All that BS that he gives out every week. He's even fooled Simon! He's full of crap and he's an average singer.'

As boos and jeers rained down on her from the audience, Cowell angrily told her to 'shut up' but Osbourne, flushed and fuming by this point, concluded, 'The public should know he's a fake!'

This was an unprecedented moment in reality pop-show history. To date, it has not been repeated either. For a judge to be so cutting and partisan as the final votes of the series were being cast was shocking and unprofessional. She later apologised, saying, 'I realised it was unfair as millions voted for him. Simon was furious afterwards.'

If her intention on the night was to prevent Brookstein from winning, it backfired spectacularly, as he won the public vote to be crowned the first winner of *The X Factor*.

Presenter Kate Thornton – who had fronted *Pop Idol* sister-show *Pop Idol Extra* on ITV2 back in the day – announced his victory and asked him how he felt. 'Shocked, shocked,' he said. 'I'm always surprised! This ain't happening. This is not happening! I do not believe it.'

He then sang 'Against All Odds' again, although, as he was so overwhelmed at winning, he made a bit of a mess of it.

In North London, Alexandra sat watching Brookstein's winning moment and dreamed that she, too, might one day win *The X Factor*.

CHAPTER FOUR

'YOU'RE GOING HOME...'

Back in 1999, before any thoughts of *The X Factor*, Alexandra had already begun to perform professionally. Ever on the lookout for ways she could help out her daughter with her ambitions, when Alexandra's mother formed her own group, Soul Explosion, she quickly found a place in the line-up for her daughter. Photographs of the band show it had a packed line-up, with up to 14 members at any given time, including French saxophonist Jean-Pierre Subra-Bieusses, drummer Dreadkey, percussionist Pete the Bongo man, who had played alongside Bell in Soul II Soul, lead guitarist Dave B, who had performed for smash-hit pop act Steps, and bassist D'andre West, who would go on to become a major figure in Alexandra's life. As for Alexandra, she was listed on the band's website as 'Alex Bell – a session vocalist on the UK scene'. She would reportedly receive around £200 for each performance.

The band focused on wedding and other corporate entertainment gigs, including conferences and product launches, and became particularly popular on the bar mitzvah and bat mitzvah circuits, belting out Jewish classic party songs like 'Hava Nagila'. They also sang soul, Latin, hip hop, jazz, country, reggae and pop. 'Just tell us about the mood and atmosphere you want to create, and we will do the rest,' read their promotional website. They built up quite a client base, including 'The Corporation of London, Merrill Lynch, The Ruling Families of Dubai and Bahrain, Black Cat Advertising Group, The Dorchester Hotel and Kasbank – Amsterdam'.

Footage of the band on the YouTube Internet website shows the band working hard onstage, performing such classics as 'Killing Me Softly', and relaxing backstage, with laughter filling the air. Onstage, Alexandra occasionally takes lead vocals with the sort of confidence and assurance one would expect of the girl who went on to win *The X Factor*. Bell works the crowd well, picking out individual audience members and asking, 'Are you having a good time, baby?'

The video was uploaded on to YouTube by someone with the username 'melissabell29'. It is not known if it is Alexandra's mother but the same user has also uploaded a video of Alexandra singing 'You Can Reach Me' by Anita Baker, at Cottons, Exmouth Market, a venue in Camden, North London. The video is undated and the footage too dark to judge when it was taken but it was clearly prior to her second *X Factor* appearance. It demonstrates that her assurance on stage comfortably pre-dated anything that she might have been taught behind the scenes on *The X Factor*, and also that her rich voice was already well developed.

During her teenage years, Alexandra worked extremely hard to chase her dream. As well as her performances with Soul Explosion, she began to put on solo performances like the one captured on YouTube.

She worked hard but it taught her a lot – not least patience. 'I was singing every weekend,' explains Alexandra. 'I had a gig every Friday, Saturday and Sunday. I earned money but not enough. But I got valuable experience from it. My worst clubs have been where nobody pays any attention – it gets depressing. I'd finish a song and they'd be so busy eating no one would clap.' These were indeed testing times for Alexandra and she was grateful for her sister's support. 'She has always been there. Every time I was low she'd talk to me. It was just because nothing was happening. I was still gigging, the gigging always helped me, because of the experience of being onstage and having the microphone in my hand, but I wanted to be recording.'

Here, Alexandra showed the sort of qualities that any aspiring star needs but it seems fewer and fewer have: patience and genuine determination. This is not the sort of determination that sees you queue for auditions and rush up to television cameras to tell them, 'Oh, my God, this means more to me than anything.' Nor is it one that makes you follow *any* route to fame, whether a dignified one or not. It is the sort of determination that makes you work hard week in, week out, and means that you are happy to do the decidedly unglamorous work. It has become a cliché, thanks to the television series *Fame*, that fame costs and that you pay with sweat. But, as with many clichés, it is true: and Alexandra paid throughout her teenage years.

It was against this background of determined hard work that Alexandra decided to audition for *The X Factor* in 2005. At her opening audition, Alexandra was clearly a little nervous. However, it was also clear that her professionalism and determination would more than see her through any nervous moments. It meant too much to her to allow her nerves to compromise her performance.

The judges saw thousands of contestants in the auditions (75,000 in total auditions but it is thought that some of these were eliminated prior to the judges being involved) and only a minute percentage were ever shown on the screen. Naturally, Alexandra was one of the contestants that were picked out for special focus. In front of the cameras, Alexandra was even more of a natural than she had been on *Star For A Night* four years earlier.

She told presenter Kate Thornton that she was into 'early Whitney and stuff'. An impressed Thornton said, 'Early Whitney? Well, I'll tell you what: it's better than early Britney!'

Alexandra giggled and said, 'Exactly!'

Thornton said, 'Whitney? That's what you aim for? Crikey!'

Then Thornton opened the door and it was time for Alexandra to face the judges. She stepped into the room, wondering what the next five minutes had in store for her and what impact they would have on the rest of her life. Emerging into the audition room itself, Alexandra looked comfortable in the high-pressure surroundings. She took her place on the giant 'X' emblazoned on the floor, took a moment to compose herself and opened her mouth to sing to the judges. She sang 'Saving All My Love For You' by her heroine Whitney Houston.

All her life Alexandra had listened to this song. It was one of the songs that had made her want to be a singer. She delivered it in a modern way, adding trills to the vocals, and there was an element of theatre to her delivery too. For instance, as she sang the line about 'resisting being last on your list', she pointed at each of the three judges in turn, who were clearly mesmerised by Alexandra.

As she finished her performance, Cowell was the first to speak. 'How old are you?' he asked. Alexandra told him she was 16. 'Amazing,' said Cowell.

'Thank you very much,' replied Alexandra graciously.

'Oh, I think you're really good,' added Cowell. With the judge traditionally considered the hardest to impress on her side, things were looking good already for Alexandra. However, there was a long way to go yet.

Next it was time for Walsh to comment. 'You look older than 16,' said the Irishman.

'I know,' replied Alexandra. 'I'm turning 17 in August.'

The judges were amused by her reply. 'Oh, *that's* it,' quipped a giggling Osbourne.

'I do get that a lot,' said Alexandra, slightly self-consciously. It was the one moment where her nerves were visible.

Cowell then decided to bring the conversation back to Alexandra's actual performance. 'One of the first times I've heard a young girl take on a Whitney song but still find a way of making it sounds current,' he said, as Alexandra shyly rubbed her nose. 'I don't normally like those trills and stuff but I thought the combination of the two styles was fantastic,' he added.

'Oh thank you very much,' replied Alexandra, seeming a little taken aback by his praise.

'I really, really liked that,' said Cowell.

Walsh weighed in again, saying, 'You did a really good job.'

Osbourne was next to speak and she chose to focus, first, on the self-assuredness of Alexandra's performance: 'Really, really confident – good voice.'

Again, Alexandra graciously responded to all this praise, saying, 'Coming from you, that means so much. Thank you.' It was time for the judges to vote on whether she would progress to the next round.

'For me, one hundred per cent it's a yes,' said Cowell. Osbourne also voted yes, as did Walsh. Cowell concluded, 'You're through. Brilliant. Well done, babe.'

Before she left the room, Alexandra was typically sweet, saying to the judges, producers and crew, 'Take care everyone.' Not for her the self-indulgent screeching outbursts that some contestants emit when they succeed. Alexandra has too much ability, manners and class for that. Her mum would have been proud of her.

Not that her progress didn't mean the world to her. Alexandra's excitement came rushing to the surface as she returned through the door to speak to Thornton. She screamed and clapped as she emerged, crying, 'Oh my GOSH!'

Thornton was delighted for her, saying, 'You're coming to boot camp!'

Comically, in the excitement, Alexandra almost seemed to have forgotten this fact and said, 'Oh yes! You'll be there all the way, will you?'

Thornton replied, 'Of. Course! These hands are for holding! That's what I'm here for.'

And now, with the formality of the interview over, Alexandra was able to start absorbing what all this meant for her. Her determined eyes filled with tears of joy and pride. She had passed the first *X Factor* test.

That evening, as the three judges flew by private jet to the next audition city, the name that was on all of their lips was Alexandra's. 'We saw a really interesting girl today,' said Walsh. 'She's got a great voice, a good attitude. I think she could have a really good career in music.'

Cowell, too, was still thinking about her. Wagging his finger, he said, 'That's one person I would very, very happily work with.'

Osbourne, too, had further contact with Alexandra in her sights. She said, 'I just think she's an amazing talent and I just hope that I get to work with her.'

But, of course, only one of the judges would get to work with Alexandra when the contestants were divided up into categories later in the series, and this episode is always entertaining, as the tables are turned for once, with the judges having to await the decision. Cowell was given the groups and was less than pleased at this news. Osbourne was happy with the category she was given – the over-25s. However, it was Walsh who was awarded Alexandra's 16–24 category, and he was delighted.

Some 200 acts were put through across the 3 categories, so it was clear that at the boot-camp stage this number would need to be whittled down, and many acts would quickly be sent home.

On the first day of boot camp, which was filmed at the Arts Depot in Alexandra's native North London, Louis gave his acts – including Alexandra – a list of five songs, from which they had to select one to perform in front of him and his team, and the other acts. These included 'Unchained Melody' by the Righteous Brothers, 'Careless Whisper' by George Michael and Christina Aguilera's 'Beautiful'. Alexandra, however, chose 'From This Moment On' by Shania Twain, and belted it out with passion and precision.

After agonising over his decision, Walsh brought them back in groups of five to learn their fate. Alexandra was one of the acts to hear that all-important yes. On the second day of boot camp, he divided his remaining acts into groups and gave each a song to learn overnight to perform the next day.

Alexandra's group also contained Nicholas Dorsett, Daniel Bywater and Richard Peachey. She worked hard and professionally to learn their song, 'End of the Road'.

For 17-year-old Dorsett, it was a fortunate song choice, as he had wowed the judges at his first audition with just that song. 'I'm just saying to myself, "This is what you have to do, go in there and just do it,"' he said.

Bywater rather messed up when it came to his turn, as he forgot the lyrics – always a fatal mistake to make on *The X Factor*. Handsome Welshman Peachey, too, had lyric problems during his performance.

As for Alexandra, she was radiating with positive attitude prior to her performance. 'If I get picked this is going to change my life, obviously. I just want to do it and show him that I'm young and I've got what it takes,' she said. Her performance was brilliant and – for many viewers – she had done more than enough to get through.

At this point, Walsh had to cut his category to just seven acts. This was an enormously tense time for all the contestants. Alexandra and the other remaining contestants were forced to wait for many agonising hours. Walsh and his team discussed the pros and cons of the acts, and then the decisions were made. The song 'You Raise Me Up' by Josh Groban played out over the screens as the news was broken to each contestant in turn. Those who were eliminated included Peachey and Bywater. When it came to Alexandra's turn, the news was good: she was through to the next stage.

The next round of the competition saw the remaining 21 contestants go to their respective judges' homes to perform. While Cowell invited his groups to his holiday home in Spain and Osbourne asked her over-25s to Beverly Hills, Walsh chose the rather less exotic surroundings of Dublin for his acts. It is always an amusing point in the series when Walsh's choice of city for this stage is in such contrast to those chosen by his fellow judges.

So it was on a plane for a short flight to Dublin for Alexandra and her fellow contestants to face fresh challenges. Which of the hopefuls would make Louis's final four acts? In the end, it came down to a choice between Alexandra and Chenai Zinyuku. Bradford-born Zinyuku, who grew up listening to the likes of Betty Wright, Aretha Franklin, Whitney Houston, Mariah Carey and Funky House, was making her second appearance on *The X Factor*. She had appeared in the first series in 2004 but was sent home in tears by Sharon Osbourne at the boot-camp stage. But, in 2005, Walsh chose Zinyuku over Alexandra.

When she was told that she was leaving the competition, Alexandra was distraught. 'From when I met you first, Alexandra, I just felt... I wasn't seeing the real Alexandra,' said Walsh. 'I felt there was something missing from you.' After the customary dramatic pause, he said, 'You're going home.'

Thornton did her best to comfort Alexandra but it was a hard task. A tearful Alexandra said, 'Right now, I just think that everything in my life has just collapsed.'

As for Zinyuku, she was through to the live finals. She had slimmed down by this point, following Walsh's comments about her weight earlier in the competition. In week one, she sang 'Hero' by Mariah Carey. The public vote left her in the bottom two along with band 4Tune, but Osbourne's casting vote – after an agonising delay from the judge – saved her. Over the following three weeks, she sang 'Young Hearts Run Free' by Candi Staton, Katie Melua's 'Closest Thing To Crazy' and Elvis Presley's 'You Were Always On My Mind'. In week four, her rendition of the Elvis song saw the public vote her in the bottom two again, where she found herself alongside fellow 16–24 act Nicholas Dorsett, and Walsh had to decide which of his two acts to send home.

He opted to eliminate Zinyuku and keep Dorsett, which seemed to come as no surprise to the female singer. 'It wasn't that difficult a decision for Louis to make,' she said. 'I always knew that, if it was down to me and one of the boys, he'd keep one of the boys because they're more likely to win. Louis has turned to me before and said, "Boys pull the votes in." He's in it to win it as well as us.' Asked how she felt about leaving the show, she added, 'It's just a bit surreal, it's surreal when you make it and it's surreal when you don't. You look forward to going home and seeing everybody, and you're a bit gutted that you've left the competition.' This setback was not about to put an end to her musical ambitions, she insisted. 'I definitely still want to go into music and I just need to figure out how I'm going to do that.' However, she later had a warning for other *X Factor* hopefuls. 'I thought everyone would love me after *X Factor* but you just don't get taken seriously.'

Meanwhile, Alexandra could only watch from home, wondering what might have been.

In some people's eyes, the remainder of the series had an element of farce to it. Chico Slimani had prompted controversy from the start of his *X Factor* journey. Simon Cowell walked out in disgust after Walsh and Osbourne voted him through at his first audition. His act had something of a cabaret element, to say the least. He was put into Osbourne's over-25s category and, at the judges'-houses stage, caused a storm when he jumped into a pool with a live microphone. Even wild rocker Ozzy Osbourne was impressed by that moment of madness. But Cowell remained distinctly unimpressed as Chico continued to progress through the show. Although Chico became something of a celebrity, and later had a number-one hit with 'It's Chico Time', it seemed unfair to Alexandra's supporters that an act such as his had progressed when she had been eliminated.

However, that is the nature of the beast with *The X Factor*. All too often talented singers are eliminated in favour of novelty acts. It is what makes it such maddening viewing at times, but also so compulsive. The nation cannot stop talking about the acts, good and bad.

The final three acts in 2005 were Shayne Ward, a pretty pop singer from Manchester, Journey South, a duo from the North East of England, and Andy Abraham, a soulful singer from Alexandra's North London.

Alexandra, watching from home, had no doubt who she wanted to win. 'I'm rooting for Andy,' she enthused. 'He's amazing. He appeals to everybody. And age doesn't take anything away. Just look at Michelle McManus. She never had the image but she won the show.'

On the night of the final, Journey South were the first to be eliminated and it came down to a face-off between Ward and Abraham, which Ward won. He went on to sing the winner's song 'That's My Goal' to rapturous applause.

As she watched Ward bask in the glory of victory,

Alexandra must have wondered how it would feel to stand on the stage as the winner of *The X Factor*. But at this point she had no immediate plans to reapply to the show. Instead, she was throwing herself into new musical projects, one of which was a performance at the 10 Room nightclub on Air Street in London's West End. With its colourful, decadent interior, 10 Room was a classy venue, even by West End standards. With its lounging atmosphere, some would say it had an almost opulent, palatial feel. And the drink prices reflected that vibe! Other *X Factor* contestants to have performed there include boy band 4 Tune. And it was another prestigious notch on Alexandra's belt to have sung in such surroundings.

However, despite such prestigious gigs, she does remember this as a tough time in her life. 'I was so unhappy – it was a low time,' she remembers. 'I used to always put myself down, I was a very negative person. I wasn't in a good place [in 2005].'

The pub-gig circuit can indeed be a crushing experience for artists, particularly those as young as Alexandra was then. Despite not being a natural in the surroundings of boozers, she nonetheless belted out some amazing performances, and drew praise and applause. Day in, day out, and week in, week out, she would be working hard, although at one point it even occurred to her that giving in was an option. 'I actually did give up,' she says. 'I was like, "I don't want to do this any more," because I thought to myself, if the one thing I love is giving me so much heartache, why am I doing it?'

Her mother confirms Alexandra's pain at the time: 'There were a lot of tears and, for a long time afterwards, Alexandra's confidence was shattered.'

But, fortunately, Alexandra's despair did not last for long. 'Music is my first love,' she said, adding that she believed music loved her in a way that a person never could.

So she picked herself up and returned to that love. As she reconnected with it, soon the relationship was being rekindled. Music had never given up on her, so she would not give up on music. She would redouble her efforts to forge a career as a professional singer. Those dreams she had carried with her were not about to be denied. This girl was back on track, and doing her best to bounce back from her *X Factor* disappointment and move onwards and upwards.

Not that she could entirely leave that reality-television experience in the past. Nor did she want to. In the aftermath of the show, she claimed, some record companies approached her, having been impressed by her *X Factor* performances. 'I have had quite a few approach me,' she said. 'We're just in talks at the moment. I'm waiting for the right deal.'

A number of viewers had criticised Walsh for not taking her through to the live shows and Alexandra was not about to go all diplomatic on us when asked for her opinion on the matter. 'I don't think they made the best choices for the finalists,' she said. Here she was not just defending herself but also the other 16-year-old contestants who Walsh had eliminated. 'They kicked out all of the sixteen-year-olds who had good potential,' she continued. 'I think Louis thought that he didn't want to have to play a father-figure role. Louis was obviously looking for a certain image. I don't know why he kicked me out. Maybe they thought, She's just sixteen, or maybe he thought I was too good for it!'

If youth was indeed an issue, it is difficult to understand why the show had made the decision to accept 16-year-old contestants. If such hopefuls were deemed inherently 'not ready', it begs the question why they were allowed to enter in the first place. This was a point made on Internet forums, at water-coolers in workplaces across the country and also on *GMTV*, with Alexandra making an appearance. 'They made a big thing out of it,' remembers Alexandra of her slot on the breakfast show. 'Everybody criticised Louis for kicking out the sixteen-year-olds. I don't know why he did that.' Here, she beat the drum for her fellow teenagers. 'He was telling some people that he thought they were too young and wouldn't be able to handle it. But there's no point in saying that the group is for sixteen- to twenty-five-year-olds, and then getting in the sixteen-year-olds, when you're going to disappoint them. They might as well just have the group from eighteen years old.'

Just three years later, she would return to *GMTV* as *The X Factor* winner.

But, despite her feisty words, Alexandra had no bitterness or regrets about her first appearance on *X Factor*. 'It was a memorable experience,' she says. 'It takes a lot of guts to do that kind of show. It either makes or breaks you. It's been really good for publicity even though I didn't make it to the finals. A lot of the times you hear that record companies don't want to approach you if you've been kicked out at this stage because they don't want rejects and they don't think people have known you enough at this stage. But I have had a lot of good feedback.'

So, overall, was she pleased with her experience? 'I'm happy I got to the stage I did,' she confirmed. However, in an ideal world, she added, she would have preferred a different judge to Irishman Walsh. 'I really wanted Simon [Cowell] to be my judge,' she said. 'I didn't think I would do well with Louis. He did say in the beginning that he had had success with boy bands. He thinks that boy bands do better, which is why he only wanted one girl.' Fair enough, but why did she think she wasn't that one girl? Again, Alexandra had a theory, saying that 'after they made such a big fuss about Chenai, how she was on the show last year and how she had had a long journey getting there and so on. They weren't going to kick her out after all of that.'

At this stage, a black person had never won a British reality pop show. But Alexandra quickly dismissed any talk that this would remain the case, or that there was any sort of racial issue there. 'They need black people in the show. Their chance of success is going to be high. Everyone has the talent. In fact, I was quite shocked when I saw so many black people in the show. Could there be a black winner? Why not? They stand as much chance as anybody else.'

Andy Abraham had not fulfilled this hope in series two but, by the time of series three, Alexandra's prediction would come true. Two years after that, she would personally fulfil her prediction – the ultimate vindication.

Meanwhile, she had her eyes set on other musical projects, one of which would see her collaborate onstage with a black artist who had done remarkably well on another British reality talent search.

CHAPTER FIVE

YOUNG
VOICES

Next up for Alexandra was a link-up with the Young Voices. For more than ten years, this organisation has been staging huge children's concerts featuring some of the most talented children in the United Kingdom. It is a major initiative with a major aim: to teach children the joys that can come from music. Not that this is the only target, for this is an ambitious affair. As Director Ben Lewis puts it, 'The hardest thing is to keep improving each year. We set ourselves high standards but making sure we satisfy everyone can be really tough. Young Voices has to be fun and exciting for the pupils, a valuable educational resource for the teachers and, finally, a great show for the parents.' To arrange these enormous children's concerts is not easy, but the feedback they receive at the end of the process makes it all worthwhile for

Lewis and his colleagues. 'My proudest moments are always reading the letters we get from our fantastic teachers, pupils and parents, telling us how valuable Young Voices is to them,' continues Lewis. 'Our office, overseen by Anne, puts in so much time and effort in order to deal with the obvious logistical nightmares that arise from such huge events and it's great to know how much it is appreciated.'

Craig McLeish arranges the musical repertoire and he gives a flavour of what the work with Young Voices might have meant to the young Alexandra. 'Young Voices is such a great way for children and young people to be introduced to performing in front of a live audience. They get the buzz of being real stars and, hopefully, the variety of the music we perform will inspire them in later years. I am so proud to be involved – I wish we'd had something like this when I was at school.'

As for those who are currently working at schools, they are in little doubt as to the benefits of the organisation's existence: the work of Young Voices has been widely praised by schoolteachers, youth workers and musical folk. Sue Haughton, choir leader of Keresforth Primary School in Barnsley, for example, says, 'Young Voices has really enhanced our music programme. Our children view this as an opportunity of a lifetime and are very excited about the concert. They have loved learning the songs and are looking forward to performing with thousands of other children as well as helping to support famous acts.'

But who are these famous acts that have gone through the doors of Young Voices? A host of stars have worked with the organisation over the years, including Chris De Burgh, Lee Ryan of Blue, Four Kornerz, Miss Dynamite, the African Children's Choir, David Gray, Michael Ball and Cliff Richard.

There have also been a handful of stars with reality-television connections who have toured with the Young Voices crew. Keith Semple will be familiar to viewers of 2002's *Popstars: The Rivals* show, as a member of boy band One True Voice. Broadcast on winter Saturday nights that year, *Popstars: The Rivals* was a reality talent contest hosted by Davina McCall, with a judging panel of pop guru Pete Waterman, former Spice Girl Geri Halliwell and music manager Louis Walsh. It produced the hugely successful Girls Aloud band, who have enjoyed 19 consecutive top-ten singles and won numerous awards. Among their number is a certain Cheryl Tweedy, who will enter Alexandra's story in due course.

One True Voice were a less successful band to emerge from the show. They were the boy band – or 'vocal harmony group', according to their testy mentor Waterman – that flopped spectacularly, despite the exposure the show had given them. They came second to Girls Aloud in the race for the post-show Christmas number one and then disbanded shortly afterwards.

It was a painful flop for all five members, but Keith Semple, the lad from Northern Ireland, picked himself up and dusted himself down in the aftermath of the One True Voice debacle. He then toured with the Young Voices crew for three years, singing a mixture of his own compositions and more familiar tunes, such as 'The Living Years' by Mike And The Mechanics. Semple, who now lives in America and has gigged in the States, looks back fondly at those days. 'My favourite tour I have ever, or will ever, be a part of,' he says of Young Voices. From One True Voice to Young Voices, it had been quite a journey for the affable and handsome Semple.

Lemar is another reality-television talent to have gone through the hallowed care of Young Voices. The North Londoner shot to fame in 2002 on the BBC1 reality show *Fame Academy*, where he won a host of admirers for his soulful performances, including a rendition of 'Let's Stay Together' by Al Green. Although he finished behind winner David Sneddon, Lemar has arguably enjoyed far more success than Sneddon has since his appearance on the show, including winning a Brit Award and enjoying numerous hit singles.

Lemar appeared with Young Voices in 2005, on the

same bill as Alexandra, and at the time, Alexandra told of how she looked up to Lemar as an inspiration of what was possible for non-winning reality-television contestants to achieve, despite not being crowned champions on their respective shows. 'Lemar is a good example of that,' she said. 'He didn't win but where is the winner now? I don't know if I would be bigger than the person who does win, but we will see.'

Both Alexandra and Lemar took part in the Young Voices' Big Sing in 2005, a hugely ambitious project which was attempting to smash the existing Guinness World Record of 83,637 young voices singing simultaneously. Among those also appearing were Joss Stone, Ms Dynamite, Keith Semple and Four Kornerz.

The song chosen for the project was 'Lean On Me', which was written and performed by the legendary American vocalist Bill Withers. It was a fitting song to represent the spirit of Young Voices, and also a song that could be said to neatly sum up Alexandra's life to date. She had known pain and sorrow but had always been wise and looked forward to tomorrow. She would, no doubt, agree that we all need someone to lean on and so will have enjoyed the performance of this particular song.

On 8 December 2005, at 2.45pm, the Big Sing kicked off in the illustrious surroundings of the Royal

Albert Hall in London. The thousands of red-T-shirted children in the Hall counted down from ten to launch the song, as children in schools across the UK lined up and waited to join in at the beginning. And as Lemar and Joss Stone began singing, so did children in schools across the country in a strictly choreographed mass singalong. It was indeed to be a big sing!

Wearing a white top and blue jeans, Alexandra looked relaxed, happy and bundles of fun on the stage. 'Make it funky, make it funky,' she sang, and she was – bopping round confidently. At the song's conclusion she smiled joyfully and licked her lips.

The event had been a huge success and was covered in the press. 1/2 MILLION KIDS SING OUT, said the *Mirror* of the record-grabbing Big Sing. Once more, Alexandra was in the media spotlight and was gaining vital experience in how to deal with the glare of attention and publicity. She had enjoyed the experience hugely. Teachers across the country, who had helped make the nationally synchronised singalong work, were also delighted. Christine Ware, a teacher at All Saints Marsh Primary School in Devon, said of her pupils, 'The children really loved the song, so it was fun. All of the children had been practising very hard and thoroughly enjoyed singing this song.'

A Big Sing representative was ecstatic, telling

reporters, 'We have had 502,000 children registered to take part in the singing. Witnesses will be signing declarations for the number of people taking part, which will be sent on to Guinness World Records.'

Not only did it smash the Guinness World Record for the largest simultaneous singalong, with over 293,978 children, it also helped some great causes. The event raised money for two charities: Clic Sargent, which cares for children with cancer, and the African Children's Choir, which helps Africa's most vulnerable children so they can help Africa in the future, both benefiting from the hundreds of thousands of pounds raised. As a generous and kind human being, Alexandra will undoubtedly have taken great pride in this fact.

As Alexandra was performing at the Big Sing at the Royal Albert Hall, a new single from Girls Aloud was rushing up the pop charts. 'Biology' was the second single released from their *Chemistry* album. Peter Cashmore, writing for the *Guardian*, described 'Biology' as 'the best pop single of the last decade'. The promotional jaunt was proving as hectic as ever for the band, including Cheryl Tweedy. As Alexandra did her best to launch a professional singing career for herself, Tweedy was busy living that lifestyle. Little did either know what was in store for them as their paths diverged to spectacular effect three years later.

Alexandra was asked by a reporter in the aftermath of the performance what her plans for the future were. She kept an open mind on another *X Factor* appearance in 2006. 'If I'm nowhere next year, I would go back on the show,' she said. 'But it takes a lot to go on that show.' As it turned out, rather than returning to *The X Factor* in 2006, she instead toured again with Young Voices. Footage of her on the tour that year shows her full of praise for the organisation and the experience it gives children. 'I think it is a very good opportunity for the kids out there,' she says. 'Firstly, it's an experience that they will only get once in a lifetime. Also, it gives them a chance to express how they want to sing. It gives them a chance to tell everyone, "This is what I want to do and I'm proud of who I am," and to come together as a community.' She also introduces herself, recounting her 2005 *X Factor* experience, which she says made her known as 'a young Whitney Houston'. Meanwhile, the accompanying footage of her singing 'Say A Little Prayer' shows that Alexandra had matured vocally and physically since her previous Young Voices experience.

She has remained hugely positive about the role that Young Voices played in her career. Alexandra is not one for the petulant rewriting of history which denies parts of her story; indeed, she is proud of where she came from and the hard work she has put into her success. She is grateful to those who helped her along the way and, far from kicking away ladders or turning up her nose, this girl holds out a helping hand and gratitude to all who deserve it. So, at the Big Sing concert at the O2 in 2008, she made a surprise appearance to tell the crowd how important Young Voices had been in her journey to the top. To an ecstatic reception from the audience, she said, 'Kids, this is for you. The reason why I've come back is that I want to let each and every single one of you guys know never to give up on your dreams ever. I performed with Young Voices three years ago and it's part of my journey. If I didn't have Young Voices, I wouldn't be the person I am today. Always follow your dreams, never give up – ever!' She has since added further praise to Young Voices. 'Being on tour with YV helped me enormously for performing on a big stage in front of a huge live audience,' she said. 'I hope that everyone has as much fun taking part with Young Voices as I did and that all the young singers around the country achieve all they dream in music.'

Another bonus for Alexandra in her Young Voices experience was the opportunity to perform alongside Joss Stone again, as she had on *Star For A Night* four years earlier. By this time, Stone's and Alexandra's careers had diverged quite drastically. While Alexandra was still aiming for the big time, Stone had arrived. She had released two multi-platinum-selling albums and been nominated for Grammys. However, the pair had remained as friendly as ever. Indeed, Stone was one of the people who Alexandra leaned on for support, inspiration and guidance. A key piece of advice that she remembers Stone giving her has stayed with her ever since: be yourself. 'Joss has been amazing to me,' gushes Alexandra. 'We've remained friends.' The two have also hung out in Stone's homes in Devon and in the USA.

Another way that Alexandra sought to boost her confidence was by joining another entertainment group, similar to Soul Explosion, called The Gilev ShowBand. The band was formed in 1995 in the shape of a keyboard/vocal partnership. As the band's biography on its website says, 'The funky duo offered the very best selection of a totally diverse music range, performed with an authentic vibe. Today, Gilev is a sensational 12–15 Piece ShowBand with more than ten years of successful performing experience, catering extensively to a variety of high-profile and celebrity audiences on both the private and corporate function circuit worldwide. It has become undoubtedly the finest ShowBand in the UK and maintains a very high ranking within the European and international forum.'

The band has enormous collective experience of performing with musical legends. Among the acts that members of the ShowBand have performed with are Tom Jones, Incognito, Van Morrison, Blur, The Streets, Craig David, Ricky Martin, Lucy Silvas, Laurence Cottal Big Band, George Michael, Steve Winwood, Sam Brown, Diana Ross, John Zone, Gorillaz, Me-yo, Diana Ross, Gloria Gaynor, Roberta Flack, Grover Washington, Kool & the Gang, Bryan McKnight, Razorlight, Tori Amos and the Lighthouse Family. The band has developed an eclectic range of sounds to its performances, which is no surprise considering that its membership is truly international, hosting no less than 11 separate nationalities including Italian, South African, Scottish, Israeli, Trini, Australian, American, South American, Austrian, North African and, of course, English. So what could someone booking the band expect for their money? The band – which played weddings, corporate events and bar mitzvahs – has an enormous repertoire from different eras, genres and national styles. The band website is bursting with positive testimonials from former clients who have booked them for a range of events and evenings.

In 2006, Alexandra became a key part of this experience as one of the seven vocalists in the Gilev ShowBand line-up. She had been spotted by the band's manager Jeremy Horowitz while performing at a separate corporate event. He was amazed by the power of her voice and asked her to join the band, which she accepted. 'When we first started working with Alexandra, we all thought, Wow, this girl's a bit special. She has an exceptional voice and an amazing stage presence but, for all her talent, she is incredibly down to earth. What's incredible for Alexandra is that she's taken her immense talent and made it on her own.'

Horowitz recalls that Alexandra was a consummate professional throughout her 100-plus performances with the Gilev ShowBand. 'No matter if she was playing to two-thousand people in Liverpool's Echo Arena or to a party of three hundred at the Dorchester, she would give it her all,' he enthused. 'She never looked down on anyone or thought she was above doing any event. The band is full of people who really enjoy what they do, and Alex was a big part of that.' Naturally, he is very proud of the part he played in her story. 'I wouldn't want to say that we built her but she is a much stronger performer today than she was two years ago,' he said in 2008. 'I have definitely noticed that she has more confidence and that is a hundred per cent because she has been performing regularly in a very high-end market, and with top singers.'

He was asked whether, following her *X Factor* triumph, he believed she might return to their fold for a performance one day. 'It's such a volatile industry, you never know,' said Horowitz. 'We have had people who have toured with major stars, who have come back. But I am sure she will do really well. It's really great news. She is a top girl.' He later added, 'It would be great if Gilev could team up with Alexandra again. We've accompanied Amy Winehouse in the past, and Alex is definitely one for the future.'

Gilev's co-director Jonni Gilbert, who spoke to Alexandra after *The X Factor* final, added, 'She really deserved to win and we are going to miss her.'

A YouTube video of the band shows them performing the song 'Mercy' by Duffy live in September 2008, and Alexandra shares the vocals with a singer called Rayla Sunshine. When Alexandra – wearing a great pink dress – starts to sing, her rich voice towers above the rest of the performance as she sings to both the audience and the camera brilliantly. Within a few months of this performance, Alexandra was singing to live and television audiences on *The X Factor*. It is clear to see she learned and polished her trade in these performances. The kind words of her band-mates and former colleagues reflect that she was a professional in every sense of the word. None of them has a bad word to say about the girl who toured with them, performing at 'weddings, parties, anythings'.

Between her performances on the party/event circuit with Gilev ShowBand and her Young Voices work, Alexandra was getting experience aplenty.

Another YouTube video from around this time features Alexandra performing the song 'Saving All My Love For You' on a theatre stage. The caption says the performance was for a Lady Carolle charity event. Carolle is a veteran of the UK music scene into which she has guided numerous acts and bands. As this video was shot, Alexandra had reportedly just performed for three hours – most likely with the Gilev ShowBand – and then turned up to support the charity event. 'You're more than welcome to wave your hands from side to side,' says Alexandra as she introduces the song. As ever, she sings the song well, almost bending right over as the soulfulness takes over.

When she is ready to end the song, she gestures with a hand movement to the keyboard player and really draws out the final line, before finishing the song to rapturous applause. 'Thank you,' she says, as she smiles and takes a bow to the audience. She then walks to the keyboardist for a high-five of celebration. Again, she exudes an aura of class, not just in her performance but in the aftermath. Her bow is graceful, her high-five with the keyboardist democratic and pleasant. This is an act without airs and graces, and with her feet firmly on the ground. Too many aspiring singing stars have fallen into the trap of assuming that, to make it big, they have to be not just fantastic singers but also huge divas, prone to tempestuous tantrums and unreasonable demands. Alexandra is far too humane and intelligent a person to ever behave this way.

As it turned out, Alexandra's touring with Young Voices meant she decided not to return to *The X Factor* in 2006. However, another young girl from London called Leona Lewis did try her luck that year, and she absolutely wowed the judges from her first audition. The then 21-year-old receptionist sang 'Somewhere Over The Rainbow' and did such a good job that the panel erupted into a round of applause at the conclusion of her performance. Not only that, the applause was led by Cowell, who said, 'That's what it's all about.'

Walsh told Lewis, 'You've got the whole package, I think.'

Cowell added, 'Well, it wasn't perfect because you fell off the melody at certain points. But when you were on, you were absolutely fantastic.'

When it came to the verdicts, all three judges plus guest Paula Abdul – who appears on the judging panel alongside Cowell on *American Idol* – emphatically put Lewis through. She was on her way. 'Well done, kid,' said Cowell.

Well done, indeed. But by the time it came to the boot-camp round, Lewis was nervous and feeling under pressure. 'I want to make myself proud,' she said. Lewis – who has often been compared with

Mariah Carey – sang Carey's song 'I Can't Live (If Living Is Without You)', before joining presenter Thornton and admitting that she didn't know if she'd done enough to get through.

Meanwhile, Cowell told his assistant judge Sinitta that 'when she's on it, she's fantastic'. When it came to the big verdict, she again sailed through to the next round –the live shows! In the first week of this round, she gave a sweet and soulful performance of 'I'll Be There' by the Jackson 5, which was one of the highlights of the evening's Motown special and rightly drew praise from the panel. Lewis was emotional as she turned to the judges for their verdicts.

'Hey, Leona,' said Walsh. 'What a fantastic way to end the first show. You know, you're a great singer, you're a class act. You look fantastic, you know. The only word of caution is, don't over-sing like Mariah Carey or Christina. Be your own voice because you have the talent to be fantastic. Well done.'

Cowell felt that Walsh was wrong to offer vocal advice to the contestant. 'How often is it in this country that somebody like you comes along because you are special. And that... that is what it's all about and, Louis, with the greatest of respect, I don't think you're in a position tonight to be offering any advice on vocals.'

Walsh confirmed that he, too, thought Lewis was 'very special'.

In week two, it was a Rod Stewart theme. Again Lewis went through in style, meaning she was free to compete in the Big Band week. Even though her voice is very contemporary, she rose to the challenge of the Big Band theme, singing 'Summertime' and giving another excellent performance.

Walsh was full of respect: 'Leona, you're a beautiful girl, you sang a beautiful song; it was an amazing performance, it was a very heart-rending performance. I think it's probably the best performance of the night, you know.'

After some horseplay between Osbourne and Cowell, the latter gave his verdict. 'Leona,' he said, 'we... ah, look, across this show, across [*American*] *Idol*, across all the other shows, let's be honest, all the girl singers we've had up to date haven't been very good. We've had a lot of dross until now. You are absolutely the best contestant I have ever had across any of these shows and that was an amazing performance.'

Lewis covered her face with a mixture of joy and embarrassment.

By the time it came to week eight, which had an ABBA theme, Lewis was already being tipped as a winner. She sang 'Chiquitita', and gave a tender and soft performance that truly hit the mark.

Walsh compared her – not entirely favourably – to Mariah Carey. 'Leona, you always do a good job,' he said. 'I thought last week you were absolutely brilliant. Tonight it was a bit like Mariah Carey singing an ABBA song. But, you know, saying that, Leona, I do think you're great and, Leona, you could be the first girl to win *The X Factor*.'

Once again, Cowell was quick to defend his contestant from Walsh's comments. 'I love Louis using, "You sound like Mariah Carey," as a negative,' he said. 'That's terrible. Leona, you know what? When I first met you, you were a very, very shy, insecure little girl. Over the last two weeks I've seen you come out of your shell. What I love about you is you're prepared to take a risk. You did not do a karaoke version of an ABBA song, which is the obvious thing to do. You made a massive attempt to do your thing on it. Once again, different league to anyone else we've heard tonight.'

Later, on the results show, Bjorn from ABBA was also highly positive about Lewis. 'Well, she's got great potential and I'm sure some day Simon will bring her into a recording studio, I'm fairly certain of that,' said the bearded Swede. 'She's got great potential, she did a very personal rendition of "Chiquitita".'

Great potential, indeed. Her confidence was growing and growing. Could she make it all the way to the final? Next, she would have to negotiate the Elton John theme week. Wearing a fetching blue dress, she sang 'Sorry Seems To Be The Hardest Word'. In the VT prior to the song, Lewis explained that performing was a dream come true for her. 'I used to wear this headset for work and when people were not looking I used to kind of pretend that I was singing at my own concert and that there were like thousands of fans,' she said. 'It is quite embarrassing but a little daydream I used to go off on sometimes... My life has changed but any time it could be "here today and gone tomorrow". I could be back sitting at my desk and just kinda daydreaming again but now it feels like I'm actually living it. I really don't want that to be taken away from me.'

She sang emotionally on an emotional night. Osbourne was quick to pick up on this mood. 'Yes, Leona, it was very emotional. You really told the story of the song so well. It was beautifully sung. Great emotion. Very, very emotional. Well done, Leona.'

Again, Cowell praised her highly, concluding, 'For every little girl who dreams about being a pop star when they are working in the office, you are... you're a role model for these people. You are special.'

However, much as Cowell's praise summed up the mood, it was the colossal applause she was receiving each week that truly reflected how well Lewis was really doing.

As the weeks went by, the judges continued to heap almost hysterical praise on to the shoulders of the superb Lewis. Walsh enthused, 'The UK has found themselves a new kind of Mariah Carey, Celine Dion, something we haven't had for a long, long time. I think you're going to be an absolute star.'

Osbourne added, 'You sang from your soul, Leona. Just mwah to you! Fantastic!'

Then, before she knew it, she was in the semi-finals and within touching distance of becoming the first woman to win *The X Factor*, and the first black contestant to do so. She sang 'Over The Rainbow' and almost ripped the roof off the studio with emotion.

Her proud mentor Cowell was overcome with emotion when he told her, 'Leona, you know, your... your lack of awareness as to how good you are is what I believe makes you such a special performer. And I will say this... for so many reasons, and I've done a lot of these shows... That was, for me, the single best performance I have ever witnessed.'

She was voted through to the final and suddenly the nation was going Leona-loopy! There she was up against Liverpudlian Ray Quinn who – with all due respect – was entertaining enough but nowhere near her quality. The result seemed a forgone conclusion before a note was sung. And once she started singing, Lewis romped home. She sang 'I Will Always Love You' by her heroine Whitney Houston, then duetted with Take That on 'A Million Love Songs' before singing Celine Dion's 'All By Myself'. Emotions were running high and the atmosphere in the studio was truly electric due to the hysteria she was creating. Here was a star, the greatest star perhaps to ever emerge from reality television.

Then it was decision time: the result of the votes would be announced and the winner crowned.

Presenter Kate Thornton prepared the finalists: 'OK, Ray and Leona, good luck to you both. The result is in.' She then told them that over eight million people had voted. 'Here is the result. The winner of *The X Factor* 2006 is... Leona!'

The winner indeed – she had charmed viewers throughout the show and romped to victory, becoming the first woman and the first black person to win a UK reality pop show. 'I'm just shocked. It's unbelievable,' she said. 'I feel like my dream has come true, the dream I've been dreaming since a little girl has come true. There were points I thought, You know what? I don't know if this is going to happen. But with the help from my friends and my family, they all kept telling me to believe in myself and keep on doing it, and I did and now I'm here, and thank you so much to them.'

She has since become arguably the most successful artist to emerge from any such show. Her debut single, 'A Moment Like This', broke a world record after it was downloaded over 50,000 times within half an hour of its release. Her next single, 'Bleeding Love', was the biggest seller of 2007 and topped the charts in more than 30 countries. Her debut album *Spirit* was a smash hit too, topping the Billboard chart in the USA, making her the first British solo artist to top the charts Stateside with a debut album. Her 5th UK single (a cover of Snow Patrol's 'Run') was the fastest-selling digital-only release of all time, after it sold 69,244 in just two days. Lewis has also been nominated for Grammy and Brit Awards, and won an Ivor Novello.

Just as crucially, she has won respect. Finally, here was an artist that *The X Factor* could be truly proud of. Her talent was undeniable and her fame global. She was, therefore, a fantastic example for any young, aspiring singer to follow. No doubt, Alexandra will have watched Lewis's rise to global fame with a mixture of emotions. She will have enjoyed Lewis's voice and admired the way she went about her quest for fame and fortune. However, a voice inside Alexandra's head might also have asked a simple question: why not me? In her 2005 *X Factor* campaign Alexandra, too, had sung with soul and beauty. She, too, had worked tirelessly to try to get to the top. She, too, had what it took to win, she believed. As she watched Lewis's glorious story, no doubt her fist will have clenched tighter and her resolve hardened. She saw herself as a distinctly different artist to Lewis, a different personality too. But she saw in Lewis a girl who had sung her way to the top. And that was where she wanted to be.

CHAPTER SIX

SHE'S BACK

It was a neighbourhood tragedy that ultimately convinced Alexandra to return and have a second crack at *The X Factor*. 'Alexandra loved our neighbour, Pauline, and when she was diagnosed with cancer we were devastated,' says Alexandra's mother Melissa Bell. 'By February 2007, Pauline had been moved to a hospice and we went to see her. She turned to Alexandra and said, "Promise me you'll enter *The X Factor* again. I'm sure you'll win it."'

When Pauline died in March, Alexandra said she was going to audition one more time. However, she was still suffering from the jolt to her confidence that her previous *X Factor* rejection had given her. 'On the day of the audition, Alexandra was shaking with nerves and was so lacking in confidence that she persuaded me to sing with her,' recalls Bell of that day at Arsenal's Emirates Stadium. 'Before we got to see the judges, we had to sing in front of the production team, who recognised Alexandra as soon as she walked in the room. After we sang, the panel started talking among themselves. They said, "We don't want your mother but could you audition in front of the judges on your own?" Alexandra looked at me but I didn't mind a bit – I could see the spark was back in her eye.'

It was time for Alexandra – alone – to face the judges proper. Visually this was a different Alexandra to the one that had left the competition three years previously. She had grown and matured. With her hair pulled back into almost a mini-beehive, and sporting a slick black shirt and jeans combo and huge earrings, she truly looked the part.

But would she *sound* the part?

Naturally, given her previous history on the show, the producers chose to give her audition special prominence on the show and, before we see Alexandra's audition, they set the scene for us. The voiceover from Dermot O'Leary says, 'One contestant waiting in the holding room knows exactly how much it means to get a "Yes".'

The camera then focuses on her, sitting looking reflective, as her voiceover says, 'My name is Alexandra. I'm nineteen and I'm from London.'

O'Leary then tells viewers, 'Three years ago,

Alexandra got down to the final seven in Louis' category.' As he says this, the footage of her at Walsh's home is shown. Alexandra is singing, with the full attention of Walsh and his assistants. He then tells her she is going home and she bursts into tears in front of Kate Thornton. 'Right now I just feel like everything in my life has just collapsed,' she tells Thornton.

The show then returns to 2008 and the new-look Alexandra, who tells viewers, 'Being on *The X Factor* the last time, it was hard because when I didn't make it through it really broke me down.' And the footage does indeed show, once more, the colossal emotional toll that Walsh's rejection took on her.

O'Leary then explains, 'It's been three years and only now has Alexandra found the strength to come back and try again.'

As she makes her final preparations for the audition, Alexandra explains how tense she feels and what she hopes the panel will observe in her. 'I'm feeling a lot of pressure at the moment. I'm more nervous than I was three years ago. I'm hoping that the judges will see a change in the past three years – and believe the change.'

Finally, the preliminaries over, scene set, it was time for Alexandra to face the judges. O'Leary gave her an encouraging pat and said, 'Now's the time. Good luck.' He opened the door and Alexandra thanked him as she stepped through it. She was accompanied by one final voiceover as she was seen walking into the room. 'It would mean the world to me if I got through because it means so much to me to be back here and show everyone what I've done in three years,' she said. 'You know I've worked very hard to better my voice so I really want to show that.' Three years of soul-searching, self-reflection and hard work – and now it came down to this.

Then she was there, in front of the judges. Immediately, they recognised the former contestant. 'Hello! We know you, right?' Cowell asked.

Alexandra nodded as she arrived at the famous 'X' on the floor. 'You know me from three years ago,' she said with a smile.

Walsh quickly chipped in to acknowledge his former mentee. 'I do! She came to Dublin. She was in my home. And she was nearly through – I didn't pick her.' He then looked into her eyes and asked Alexandra, 'Do you really want this badly?'

Ask a silly question, Louis!

'I want this... so badly,' said Alexandra with palpable emotional intensity. 'Words are indescribable how much I want this. I've learned a lot in the last three years that I've been away and grown up as a person.'

To even the most detached viewer, it was clear that this was a pivotal moment for Alexandra. Anyone watching would be already caught up in the emotion she was feeling as she embarked on her second quest for *X Factor* glory. This was her moment to put behind her the ghosts of her previous appearance. Her chance to show just how great she was, how great she had become.

'Off you go,' said Walsh.

Before starting to sing her song, Alexandra took a few moments to compose herself. She was not about to rush into this vital performance and blow it. She wanted to make sure she was ready. Perhaps, in those final moments before she opened her mouth to sing, she took the time to remind herself how hurt she was when she was rejected by the show in 2005. This time, she told herself, I *will* make it. Just as in 2005, she sang Whitney Houston's 'Saving All My Love For You'. Vocally, the 2008 Alexandra was in a different league to the 2005 version. Back then she had been marvellous but this time she was magnificent. Her voice had added richness and – unsurprisingly – maturity. This time, too, her delivery was more traditional. Most of all, though, her performance was awesome.

The effect it had on the judges was obvious from the start. Cheryl Cole nodded knowingly at Dannii Minogue, then Walsh looked at Cowell, who nodded happily at him. As the performance proceeded, Minogue began to shake her head in disbelief. Could a girl this young be producing such a rich, soulful performance? Cole, too, was blown away, whispering to Minogue that Alexandra's voice was giving her goose-bumps.

As her verse and chorus came to an end, it was time for Alexandra to receive the judges' verdict. What would they make of their returning contestant? Cowell was the first to speak. 'Thank you,' he said. 'I've just *got* to ask Louis: what did you think?'

Walsh was impressed – and then some. 'I thought you were amazing,' he told the returning Alexandra. 'Absolutely amazing, Alexandra. In every sense, I think you're world class. Look at her! She's like a diva now! She's fantastic.'

At this point, the intensity of Alexandra's ambition came to the surface as she broke into tears in response to Louis's praise. She tried to compose herself but found it hard to speak. 'This... means so much to me, you don't understand,' she said with her voice trembling.

If one person in the room did understand Alexandra's feelings, it was Cheryl Cole, who had tears in her eyes too as she gazed knowingly at the girl in front of her, feeling her pain and ambition deeply. Cole shared the burning intensity of Alexandra's focus. She, too, struggled to speak when it came to delivering her verdict. 'I was just blown away,' she managed to say. She and Alexandra both laughed, trying to release the intense emotions they were feeling. Cole continued, 'I think you're amazing. I've got goose-bumps. You were born to sing and you're absolutely gorgeous.'

Alexandra was gracious and polite in response. 'Thank you very much,' she said. 'Thank you so much.'

Dannii Minogue said simply, 'It was amazing.'

Alexandra said, 'Thank you. Thank you very much.'

But what would the king of the panel, Simon Cowell, say? It is still his approval that most contestants seek. To say he approved would be an understatement. 'Well, Alexandra, I thought Louis made one of the most stupid decisions because of how rare is it for a young girl like you to be able to walk in and sing like that,' he said. It was not just her voice that met with his approval. 'You've got a great personality. The best audition I've seen today.'

At this final piece of praise, Alexandra gasped and said, 'Oh, my God.' But there was more joy to come for her as Cowell asked, 'And you know what, Alexandra? I don't think we've even heard the best of you by a mile.'

Would the judges put her through to the next round? Well, given the effusive praise, it seemed a foregone conclusion but, as is the nature of the show, the producers created as much drama as they could. The Westlife/Mariah Carey version of the song 'Against All Odds' chimed into the show's soundtrack.

'Louis, yes or no?' asked Cowell of his fellow judge.

The Irishman replied, 'One hundred per cent yes.'

Cole was next up with her decision and was similarly unequivocal. 'It's not even a question in my eyes,' she said, 'A hundred per cent yes.'

Minogue, too, said yes, which left only Cowell. He said, 'Alexandra? We'll see you in the next round.'

As she burst through the doors, Alexandra whispered with joy, 'I got through!'

O'Leary was delighted for her and said, 'Yaaay!'

Once more she broke down. 'I'm just so grateful! Nobody understands what this means to me,' she said.

Back in the audition room, the judges were still discussing her. 'She's in a good space now,' said Walsh.

Cowell agreed, adding, 'I love her.'

Even at the close of play, they were still full of praise for her. Minogue told the cameras that Alexandra was her favourite auditionee of the day.

Cole agreed, saying, 'She was mind blowing. She's got something special.'

Meanwhile, Cowell said he was relieved that the show was going to get a second chance with Alexandra. 'I can't believe we nearly lost a talent like Alexandra. Thank God she's come back.'

And she had come back in some style. The early signs were that this time she would not be denied so easily.

Her mother was one of the first to greet Alexandra and she clearly remembers an experience that day. 'I went with Alex to the first auditions at the Emirates Stadium and, as she was being interviewed by the host, Dermot O'Leary, I watched her sitting there among the hundreds of contestants, looking so demure and mature. I collared Dermot's private runner and said, "Excuse me. Do you see that girl being interviewed by Dermot? She's your winner. Her name's Alexandra Burke. I want you to remember this moment and, when she wins, I want you to call and apologise for looking at me like I'm completely crazy."'

It is worth considering just how few contestants on reality-television shows have failed in one series and then come back and made a genuine success of their second attempt. Most times, the more they keep returning, the more unequivocal the rejection gets. For instance, Matt Johnston of One True Voice – the band formed from ITV show *Popstars: The Rivals* (which, of course, also included Alexandra's Young Voices colleague Keith Semple) – came back for a second go after the flop of that band. Pitching up in series one of *The X Factor*, he was full of determination that he would make it this time. However, the judges were less than impressed with him. He scraped through into the second round but was then sent home. For a young man who had finished as the boy with the highest votes on *Popstars: The Rivals*, it was a bitter blow. Prior to this, he could perhaps have consoled himself that his failure after that show had been due to bad luck. Now, with a second flop, that possibility seemed more remote.

An even more bitter experience befell Nikk Mager in series five of *The X Factor*. Mager has a long history with reality television – albeit not a particularly happy one. He auditioned on the first series of *Pop Idol*, only making it as far as the final 50. Indeed, probably his most memorable legacy from the show was being compared visually with *EastEnders* character Robbie Jackson, which is far from flattering. However, it seemed he hadn't had enough yet. He next auditioned on *Popstars: The Rivals* and this time he got as far as the live finals. However, he failed to make the top five boys who were automatically picked for the boy band and, instead, he joined the unofficial 'runners-up' band called Phixx. Although they had some chart success, it was fleeting and Mager found himself singing to small audiences at working-men's club, a million miles from where he wanted to be in every sense.

So in 2008 he decided to try the reality-television route again, perhaps believing it would be third time lucky. Instead, this time he was to receive the most direct and crushing rejection of his life. Naturally, much was made on the show that he had previously

Where it all began for Alexandra – Copenhagen Primary School in Islington.

© Rex Features

Above: Fans gather to support their favourite *X Factor* contestant.

© *Rex Features*

Below: Alex performs with Ruth Lorenzo at the switching on of the Oxford Street Christmas lights in 2008.

© *Getty Images*

Alexandra performing at an *X Factor* secret gig in December 2008.

© *Getty Images*

Above: Fellow contestant Diana Vickers with Alexandra.

Below: Eoghan Quigg, Alexandra Burke, Diana Vickers and JLS prepare for a secret *X Factor* gig in London's Oxford Street.

© *PA Photos*

Alexandra at her homecoming performance.
© *Getty Images*

Alex looking gorgeous at the Wireless Festival in Hyde Park.

© Getty Images

Celebrating a fantastic, life-changing win.

© *Mirrorpix*

At the Brit Awards in
February 2009. How
long before she wins
an award herself?

© Rex Features

auditioned on the same show as Cole, who was now a superstar pop act and a judge. 'It's weird for me and I'm sure it'll be weird for her,' said Nikk. 'Six years later she's in the biggest girl band in the country and I'm playing working men's clubs; I fit in between the bingo.'

Having finished his performance, he was told by Walsh, 'I honestly don't think you have a great voice; you're a nice guy but you won't win this competition.' Already, things were looking bad. Walsh had judged Mager in *Popstars: The Rivals* and, if even he was not willing to show a bit of 'old times' sake' support, what hope did Mager have from the rest of the judging panel?

He soon found out. Next, Minogue delivered her verdict. It proved to be even more damning. 'Your voice isn't strong enough to get through the competition and you look too old to fit into a boy band. I would struggle to place you,' she said. Ouch! And Cowell had yet to speak!

He rounded up proceedings by telling Mager, 'OK, I can make this straight forward, the competitions have gone up and you haven't got "it", and it's time to stop chasing this dream and do something you'll be happy in and not frustrated. It's gone on long enough now and I can tell you by that audition you haven't got it in your voice, and I don't think you ever will.'

Mager seemed crushed. Cole refused to judge her

former co-auditionee and instead gave him a hug. But it was a less than ideal response as, by refusing to judge his performance, the message she gave out – possibly unintentionally – was that she was rejecting him but couldn't bring herself to say it. Indeed, ironically, Cowell was probably the kindest of the bunch. His advice was direct but humane and Mager would do well to follow it.

But initial signs suggested he would. Having failed on three different occasions to get what he wanted from reality pop shows, he emerged defiant and still convinced he could make it. 'They obviously didn't get me, which is cool,' he said with a shrug. 'I respect their opinions. But I'm not going to give up. I want this too much.'

Despite a combination of public votes and judges' comments rejecting him over three series, he insisted he was not finished. 'There is something else out there for me – there is something just around the corner,' he declared. Most contestants, successful or not, eventually accept that Cowell knows what he is talking about. Not Mager, it seems. 'Everyone dreads the kind of comments Simon Cowell gives – and he told me it was my opportunity to give up. But Simon has said numerous things about numerous people. He said Mika would never have a chance in hell of making it, and he was the biggest-selling artist in 2007.'

His defiant speech was not finished. 'Gary Barlow, he said, was never going to amount to anything. Look how big Take That are right now. If I put my name on that list then, yeah, it's positive. That's cool. I'll take my chances. After all, Madonna was Rejection Queen. You don't get anywhere if you're going to give up, do you? So yes, I'm gutted but there is lot to look forward to. I've got a bright future ahead.' He was last heard of as he prepared to perform at a small festival in Norwich. 'I'm really, really excited about this,' he said. 'It's a good gig. There should be about ten thousand people there. I think I'm going to be one of the headliners because *The X Factor* was so huge.'

But his defiance could not mask the heartbreak he showed during the judges' comments after his audition. He clearly wanted it so much and believed he could be a star, and it was precisely because he'd been rejected before that it seemed to hurt so much. So it seems that, far from getting easier each time, the knockback only hurt more.

It was precisely this sort of scenario that Alexandra was seeking to avoid when she returned. Instead, she would have been hoping for something closer to what happened to perhaps the most memorable comeback kid of reality pop shows – Darius Danesh. Scot Danesh rose to fame in the first major reality pop show of modern times – *Popstars*. There, the ponytailed, goateed singer became the most memorable contestant of the lot, for all the wrong reasons. Tall, charismatic and eccentric, he was the butt of many jokes on and off the show. His spellbinding self-belief all too easily spilled over into over-confidence and arrogance.

Then came his cringe-making Britney moment. Danesh chose to sing the Britney Spears hit 'One More Time' to the judges. His a cappella performance was extraordinary, swooping to the highest and the lowest of notes within the space of a few seconds. With exaggerated hand movements and totally over-the-top drama, it was a truly bizarre performance. Judge 'Nasty' Nigel Lythgoe summed it up later: 'You did the most extraordinary thing.'

The Scot was sent home from the competition but, before leaving, told the judges that he would have a multi-platinum-selling album within years. What he had more immediately was a nation mocking him. The press had picked up on him early in the show's broadcasting and had made him not just a figure of fun, but almost a figure of hate. These were tough times for Danesh, who would have had little idea how big *Popstars* was going to become when he first auditioned, as this was the first major reality pop show on television. Looking back since, he has been philosophical: 'I was brilliantly naive and very over-enthusiastic.'

However, his self-belief and focus saw him return to

the fray the following year on the subsequent ITV show, *Pop Idol*. He made it through to the final 50, despite being called 'cheesy' by the panel. He was then voted off by the public but, thanks to a twist of fate, this was not the end of the story. Fellow contestant Rik Waller had to drop out because of a sore throat. So Danesh – who finished behind Waller in the voting – was brought back. By this time, the facial hair had gone, the hair had been cut and he looked like a new man. The public warmed to the comeback kid and voted him through week after week. However, he exited the show at the semi-final stage, leaving Will Young to defeat Gareth Gates in the final.

Not that Danesh was complaining, as he felt he should not have triumphed. 'If I'd won, I would have been the biggest nightmare. I wouldn't have fitted the mould. If I'd won, either the *Pop Idol* logo or I would have imploded. I have to be the person I am.' Indeed, he could have signed on to the *Pop Idol* bandwagon even having not won, but chose not to. 'I had to make the decision to release a cover single off the momentum of *Pop Idol* or release original music. I thought, if I did it off the show, the success would not have been about me. Doing a cover would have been easy but it is not about shifting records, it's about the music.'

Since then, it has been all go for the man they call 'the cat with nine lives'. He had his platinum-selling album with *Dive In*. He then released a second album, *Live Twice*, before embarking on a career in musicals, including *Chicago*, *Guys and Dolls* and *Gone With The Wind*, in which he played Rhett Butler, and was praised by reviewers. One wrote, 'The diabolically dashing Darius Danesh brings a seductively insolent charm, a dark velvet voice and a genuine fugitive pathos to the cynical blockade runner.'

However, stories such as these are rare in the annals of reality-television history. Usually, when you've been shown the door in that format, that is the end of the line as far as fame and fortune via the television route goes.

Therefore, one can understand Alexandra's nerves as she returned to *The X Factor* – and her unbridled joy when she got through her first audition. However, there was still a very long way to go and, before she could even think about further progress, Alexandra had to contend with a family drama that – but for her intervention – would have turned into a family tragedy.

CHAPTER SEVEN

'I'M DIALLING 999'

Just before Alexandra left home for the boot-camp stage, her mother fell ill and it is no exaggeration to say that Alexandra saved her life. Bell picks up the story: 'The night before, I had gone to bed feeling tired and ill, and on the Sunday morning I just couldn't get up,' she recalls. 'I assumed that it was flu because I didn't even have the energy to lift my head from the pillow. Alexandra came in and sat on my bed. She said, "Mum, you need to see a doctor," but I disagreed. She wanted to call an ambulance but I was insistent she should do no such thing, saying, "I'm not that ill. I don't want to waste NHS time."

'But Alexandra said, "Mum, you've turned as white as a sheet – and you're a black woman. I'm dialling 999." With that, she left the room. Then I remember being lifted into the ambulance. When I arrived in casualty, I was surrounded by a team of doctors. There, in the background, I could see all my other children and then I started to lose consciousness.'

Alexandra had acted in the nick of time as, had there been any further delay, her mother might well have died. Bell says that her offspring were wonderfully supportive in the weeks that followed too. 'For two weeks the children stayed by my side, not knowing if I'd survive,' she says. 'At one point, I opened my eyes and saw about twenty-five doctors, all shaking their heads. I don't know how Alexandra coped. One minute she was a young girl getting ready for boot camp, the next she was worrying her mother might die and trying to be strong for her younger brother.'

Once more the steely, determined nature of Alexandra came to the fore as she combined trying to become the mother of the family while her real mother lay recuperating, and continuing on her *X Factor* journey.

And the beginning of that long journey was the notorious boot-camp phase. It is at this stage of the competition that the contestants get a reality check. After the joy of getting through the first phase, suddenly they are faced with a whole new challenge. The boot-camp sees contestants slashed from the competition with ruthless efficiency. With the brutal sorting out of the rough from the smooth, this is where it gets real.

As Alexandra looked round the talent on show at boot camp, she wasn't at all sure she would make it past this hurdle. 'The girls seem really strong. I feel like it's the strongest I've ever seen on *The X Factor* girls-wise and that is my category. That's what is making me even more scared. I feel like I stand no chance. It's not the same as it was three years ago. Talent grows in this world and the show has grown.' The show was broadcast over two nights that weekend as a double-bill. As Cowell put it, 'This is the time when we realise whether we've actually got anyone decent or not.' Alexandra would soon answer that question comprehensively.

Dermot O'Leary introduced the show with the telling comment, 'Welcome to *The X Factor*, where it's time to ramp up the pressure. Thousands have auditioned all over the country and the best have been brought here to London to see if they've got what it takes to move to the next stage of the competition.'

In fact, some 182,000 had applied for the auditions originally and, by this stage, there were just 150 remaining. As these contestants were driven in coaches to the venue, they told the camera how they felt and Alexandra admitted, 'I'm very, very, very nervous.'

With all the contestants gathered in the prestigious O2 venue, Minogue told them, 'One of you is going to be this year's *X Factor* winner.'

Cowell told them he was expecting some incredible

performances. 'You are going to perform one song and we're going to decide straight after that performance whether you are staying or going.' Each act would take to the stage in groups of five, perform a song and then wait for the verdict from the judges.

Cole told them that, having stood on that stage and performed herself, she wished them all the best of luck.

Alexandra – who would make a triumphant return to the O2 venue six months later – was quite right to identify 2008 as a peculiarly strong year for female contestants, and Lancashire-born Diana Vickers was one of the strongest of the field. The 17-year-old, born in Lancashire, had previously taken part in local singing competitions but had never performed her own concert or sung professionally. However, from the start she seemed to stand out, due in part to her quirkiness. Then there was Laura White. She started singing at the age of six and then learned the piano and clarinet at nine. At 15 she started gigging, including a residency at a hotel, singing jazz classics. Joelle was another incredible contestant in her first audition, quickly prompting hopes that here was 'the next Leona Lewis'. She sang 'I Have Nothing' beautifully and wasn't even put off her stride when Cole interrupted to ask her to look at the judges as she sang. Among the older female contestants, too, there was talent aplenty. Mum-of-five Rachel Hylton wowed the judges at her opening audition with a performance of 'You Know I'm No Good' by Amy Winehouse. She would be another strong contender, although she was older than Alexandra and thus in a separate category. The same was true of Spanish songstress Ruth Lorenzo. So across two age groups, the female talent was exceptional. Little wonder Alexandra was nervous.

Wearing a white vest, short black skirt and white high-heeled shoes, Alexandra looked fantastic as she said, 'I wanna do well, I really wanna make it further than I did the last time. But I just don't feel it's gonna happen this year. But I really want it to.'

She sang 'The First Time Ever I Saw Your Face'. Originally written in 1957 by folk singer Ewan MacColl, it has since become a much-covered and popular song. Among those to sing it are Celine Dion and Leona Lewis, and Alexandra's boot-camp performance was on par with those artists' versions. The theatre was enraptured by her.

Simon Cowell smiled proudly as she sang, and gave his fellow judges knowing glances. Louis Walsh took a sip from his drink but that could not for a moment mask the admiration that was written over his face. Meanwhile, behind Alexandra, the four contestants who had taken to the stage with her were nodding enthusiastically as they listened to her voice, waiting for their own turn to sing.

As she finished singing, Cowell looked full of joy. The audience – made up of her rivals, remember – gave Alexandra a standing ovation. She looked taken aback, both by this and by how well she had performed. 'Thank you so much,' she mouthed to the appreciative audience, tears forming in her eyes before she gave them a bow.

Walsh was the first of the judges to speak. 'Alexandra, that was absolutely great,' he said. 'Faultless, faultless audition. I think you've improved incredibly.'

She thanked him for his remarks.

Cole, meanwhile, still appeared to be experiencing a profound physical reaction to Alexandra. 'My body was covered from head to toe in goose-bumps,' she said. Alexandra smiled at this news as Cole added, 'You were born to do this.'

Summing up the strength of the field, Minogue said, 'It is insane what we have seen today and you're one of the really good ones. Loved that.'

Cowell – ever willing to ham it up a bit – said, 'You... are... incredibly mature. Fantastic potential. You know what's really exciting? We still haven't seen the best of you yet.'

She was shocked by this, gasping and saying, 'Oh, God!'

After the nervous wait for the judges to confer, they finally made their decision. Walsh smiled to Alexandra and said, 'You're through to the next round.'

It was hardly a shock given the overwhelmingly positive remarks the judges had made. But all the same, Alexandra was overjoyed and came bursting through the door to embrace Dermot O'Leary. 'I got through!' she said. 'My mum will be so proud! Oh, my God!'

O'Leary embraced her once more and said, 'Well done, you!' She then said she was shaking with shock.

One more hurdle had been negotiated and in a very tough year – could the tide be turning for Alexandra? But it was going to be a competitive field in Alexandra's category, as also through were strong contenders Diana Vickers and Laura White.

'I want this,' she said with tears in her eyes again. It was proving to be an incredibly emotional journey for her. 'This is all I want and if it takes having to keep coming back then I will.'

She sang Mariah Carey's 'Hero', a song that was to take on enormous significance later in the competition. Once more, the judges were entranced by her magnificent vocals, although she still had to wait while the judges decided who had made it through to the next round. Eventually, she was called to the stage alongside other contestants, including Diana Vickers and Eoghan Quigg.

'It's been the hardest we've ever, ever, ever done this,' said Cowell.

Walsh added, 'We can only pick the people we absolutely believe in... you're all coming back.'

The contestants jumped for joy and then fell into a celebratory group hug.

Cowell then told them, 'You are all potential winners.'

As she celebrated outside, Alexandra said, 'I'm in shock!'

Then it was the time for the producers to decide which category each judge would get to mentor for the remainder of the competition, and it was the judges who had to sit and wait to find out.

Minogue said, 'The girls are pretty strong, they are pretty good this year. I want the girls!'

Walsh, meanwhile, said he preferred to get the boys or the groups, adding, 'I don't want the over-25s this year.'

Cole also preferred to avoid the elder category. 'If my phone rings now and I've got the "overs",' she said, 'this competition might be over because I don't see any point in going forward.'

Cowell, meanwhile, wasn't sure about the boys category.

'The problem with the guys,' he said, 'is that they're very young this year. I think I should get the young girls category because I think I know who the stars are in that category.'

Cowell was the first to be called by the representative of the producers and he got the boys. 'I'm thrilled for them more than me,' he said.

Then Minogue was told that she had the over-25s category. She seemed remarkably pleased by this news, considering that a few minutes earlier she had been clear how much she wanted the girls.

Walsh, who was called next, urged the producer to 'put me out of my misery'. On hearing he'd been given the groups, he said, 'I'm happy, yeah, I'm happy!'

So this left one judge (Cole) and one category (the girls), and, on being told her category, Cole screamed with joy. 'I am a very happy judge right now,' she said.

So it would be Cole who would be mentoring Alexandra.

Then came the normal banter between the judges. Cowell phoned Walsh to 'commiserate' with him and to jokingly console him that it is 'not the winning but the taking part' that counts. 'Simon Cowell is so pompous,' moaned the Irishman.

Then Cole rang Cowell and said, 'Please try not to cry – I got the girls!' When he replied that he got the boys, Cole blew a raspberry down the phone at him.

At this point, Alexandra was quite unaware of which judge would be mentoring her category. But she knew that she had got through the boot-camp stage and was, therefore, in with a huge chance of progressing to the live shows. The judges'-houses round was always a tense time for X *Factor* contestants – and, of course, more so for her than most because that was the stage at which she had exited the competition previously. She was told that she would be flying to luxurious Cannes in the south of France for the next round, from which she would have no doubt realised that it was unlikely that she would be being mentored by Walsh again, as he traditionally takes his category to his hometown of Dublin. However, all she – and her fellow contestants – could do was speculate, as they still had no definite idea who was going to be their mentor.

Cannes is a destination of immense glamour and opulence. Situated on the French Riviera, it has wealth etched into it wherever you look. Luxury mansions, glorious yachts and expensive shopping boutiques are plentiful. The locals are rich and so are the visitors. Every summer the film world flocks to Cannes for the annual Film Festival. So one way or another, this is a city that positively glitters with the sort of wealth that a successful show-business career can bring. As Alexandra and her fellow contestants arrived at the nearby Nice Airport, they would immediately have been struck by the beauty of the French Riviera. Cannes is a pleasant drive from posh Nice with its splendid Negresco hotel, and this drive will have only served to increase the determination of the contestants to make it big, to taste the riches so plainly on show in areas such as this.

When they arrived in the vicinity of the audition locations, they were shown to a gorgeous holiday home with the sun blazing down on a swimming pool and palm trees. They were assembled beneath a balcony, from which their judge would appear. Nervously, they waited. Each will have had their own preferences as to who would – and would not – be their judge. Finally, the waiting was over. Wearing a straw hat, Cole ran to the front of the balcony and waved at her contestants. They, too, were excited and cheered, whooped and jumped up and down in celebration. There was more excitement when Cole's band-mate Kimberley Walsh then appeared on the balcony. The Girls Aloud pair would work together at this stage of the competition.

'This is a proper little girl-fest,' said *Xtra Factor* presenter Holly Willoughby when the contestants and Girls Aloud pair sat together in the shade. All the girls agreed with Willoughby's view that it was nice to not have 'scary Simon' there. Cole added that she was glad that Cowell was not there offering his opinion. 'It's my own opinion,' she said.

Kimberley Walsh told them, 'We have been there and, for me, I found it really difficult under the pressure.'

Cole advised the girls to not allow their 'nerves to

take over', but she got quite emotional at the end of the day. Having been through the reality-television experience herself in the past, she took the responsibility she had as a judge very seriously. She realised she was dealing with people's dreams, the same ones she had had on her reality show. Hers had come true but she was not going to be able to wave a magic wand and make all the contestants' dreams come true.

She broke down while talking with Willoughby. 'Today has made me realise the responsibility I've got,' she said with a sniff. When asked how close she was to a decision, she said, 'I've got a fair idea.' She explained that she had four in mind for the finals. Of course, she would only be able to take through three.

As for Kimberley Walsh, she said, 'It's too much responsibility, especially because we've been there before. We know how they feel. We've been there and it's awful.'

They then joked about how beautifully Cole cried. 'Only Cheryl Cole could cry diamonds,' said Willoughby.

There were to be plenty of tears all round the following day. Cole had overnight to make her decision and then she would have to tell each contestant individually whether or not they had got through to the next round – the live finals. Just as sports people say that it is far more painful to lose a semi-final than a final, so too do *X Factor* contestants insist that the judges'-houses stage is the worst time to leave the show. Having come so far and begun to taste the luxury that fame can bring them, it is terribly harsh to then be sent home. Alexandra knew this better than any of the contestants there, having had just that experience in 2005. No wonder O'Leary told the camera that, though he thought the girls category was going to be so strong, the nerves had really got the better of them. 'Some of them just crumbled,' he added.

Would Alexandra crumble or rise?

She was the last to perform. 'This is a really tough group,' she agreed. 'I mean the talent here today is absolutely phenomenal. I don't want to go home to say "no" again. I'm in North London... in Islington in a council flat. I share a bed with my sister. Winning this show would completely change my life drastically.'

She sang the Beyoncé track 'Listen' and, from a gentle start, she built the vocals as the song progressed and was really belting them out beautifully by the end. Cole seemed breathless with admiration at the end and thanked Alexandra, who then skipped off up the stairs to rejoin O'Leary for an interview.

'That's the biggest soundtrack song,' said Cole, 'and she kills it like that.' Cole then wondered out loud why she had so hoped for the girls. 'It's the hardest category,' she said, reflecting how many potential winners there were among the girls.

It was going to be a long night for Cole as she decided who to take through to the live finals. As she went over and over in her mind who deserved to make the cut, she remembered how she felt when her future was being decided by judges on *Popstars: The Rivals* all those years ago. She would have loved to give all of them a break but knew that was not possible. All the same the responsibility of her position weighed heavily on her as she went over and over her decision.

Meanwhile, Alexandra, too, had a difficult night. She had performed 'Listen' brilliantly but, knowing that she had done all she could to convince Cole, was both a blessing and a burden. Had she done enough? Would she make it to the live finals, where huge television audiences would watch her and vote for whether she should continue?

As dawn broke on decision day for the girls, everyone concerned with the decision was nervous. Cole and all the contestants woke with butterflies in their stomachs. Alexandra will have felt immensely nervous. It was going to be an emotionally fraught day. Cole sat in a shaded gazebo, donned her cowboy hat and waited for each of the girls to come forward so she could break the news to them. She would speak to six girls in total, but only three would make it through.

First to come was Anastasia Baker. She had made a mistake in her song and positively broken down on set as a result. She later blamed this on post-natal depression, saying, 'I just lost it. The nerves got to me and the other girls didn't help. It was very bitchy behind the scenes.' So on the day, it was no surprise to her when she was told she had not made it through to the live shows.

'You absolutely fell apart in front of my eyes and that would be a worry for me,' said Cole. 'I have to make the decision. I can't take you any further. I'm *so* sorry.' It was little surprise to anyone, including the viewers.

Hannah Bradbeer had been a favourite throughout the show to this point, ever since she sang 'Mercy' by Duffy at her first audition. She was next to get the Cole verdict. 'I just want you to know that this decision I've made has been the hardest I've had to make,' said Cole. 'I've had loads of positives and negatives for everybody.' After a lengthy dramatic pause, Cole announced, 'I'm so sorry, honey, I have to let you go home. I'm so sorry.'

A devastated Bradbeer refused to take part in a post-verdict interview with O'Leary. 'No I'm going home,' she said curtly and strolled past him.

With two 'nos' already delivered, surely Cole would be delivering a 'yes' soon?

But, as Diana Vickers took the nervous walk to

Cole, she had no idea what the verdicts had been so far. As is traditional on the show, Cole managed to heavily imply that Vickers was out, before delivering the good news.

'I do think you've got a really unique talent,' she said. 'Much as I love you, and get you, I don't know if the public would get the quirkiness.' It seemed all was lost for Vickers. However, Cole then smiled and told her, 'You're one of my three!'

Vickers held her face in shock and gasped, 'Oh, my God!' The pair fell into a joyful cuddle and Vickers whispered, 'I love you!'

As the happy contestant skipped off, Cole told her to scream, which she did. As she bounced up the stairs to speak to O'Leary, she said, 'Oh, my God, oh, my God, oh, my God!' O'Leary hugged her and called her 'sweetheart'. She then rang her mum and delivered the good news.

Would Laura White be left with a smile on her face too? Before approaching Cole, she told the cameras, 'I feel like I've come such a long way in such a small space of time, really. I've really started to believe in myself. I really hope I've done enough.' It was time to find out.

She sat down next to Cole, took a deep breath and waited to learn her fate. Had she made the final three of the category? 'You know I've loved you from day one,' said Cole. 'I've watched you progress from the first audition. I think you've got amazing potential. But the problem I've got is, you are *so* specific as an artist. You have such a specific sound that I don't really know if the public would be able to relate to that. I have made a decision.' White could be forgiven for assuming she was about to be shown the door. However, Cole then told her, 'You're going to have to be in my final three!' She was understandably shocked, as well as delighted. Cole reminded her that she should be feeling joy, saying, 'I'm so happy! You're in the final three!' More joy as another place was taken.

But would there still be one left by the time Alexandra joined Cole for the verdict?

It was time for Amy Connelly – who reduced Cole to tears in her first audition – to face the music. Her mother had died of breast cancer when Connelly was just seven years old and this story, and her performance, had moved Cole and the viewers at the start of her *X Factor* journey. That journey had, said Connelly prior to receiving Cole's verdict, been 'a life-changing experience'. The mentor told her contestant that she really believed in her. 'From the first time I saw you, you just make me melt,' she said, holding Connelly's hands. 'There is something about you that is so genuine. I do genuinely think you've got something special. But I can only take three people through to the live finals.' After a long and – for

Connelly in particular – agonising delay, Cole said, 'I'm so sorry, Amy, I can't take you through to the next round. I'm so sorry.'

The distraught Scot was shown phoning her father and apologising for not getting through.

So attention turned to Alexandra. Having fallen at precisely this hurdle in 2005, she was the most nervous of the lot. True, her performance the previous day had been world class by any standards, but then she had been confident in 2005 too. So she could take nothing whatsoever for granted. 'I'm frightened, man,' she said. 'I don't want to be told "no". I don't want to go through what I went through again. I just don't want to go home and say "no", not again.' She continued her pre-verdict interview by making a plea. 'I am more than ready for this now,' she insisted. 'I want 2008 to be my year. I really want someone to get where I'm coming from and understand how much I want this.' Alexandra's voice then went into a whisper as she said, 'This is my dream, man. I don't want anything else. I want this.'

She took a deep breath, stood up and made her way to Cole, where her verdict would be delivered. Memories came flooding back of her disappointment three years before. Would Cole repeat what Walsh had done and send her home? Could it be that this was her level; that the judges'-houses round was as far as she could get? 'I know you've been through this before, and I loved you from the moment I saw you,' said Cole. 'The first audition – I was blown away,' she added. However, the sentiment then took a turn for the worse, as Cole appeared to be preparing to eliminate Alexandra from the competition. 'I don't know if you wear your heart on your sleeve,' she said, and a worried expression fell across Alexandra's face. 'When I listen to you, you are so amazing. But you know as well as I do that, when it comes to the public vote, they're going to have to know the real Alexandra.' At this point, Alexandra – and the viewing public – were on a knife-edge. Cole was about to deliver an even more troubling sentence. 'I really didn't want to be the person to do this to you again. But I've had to make the decision.'

Alexandra gasped and looked stunned. *Again?* She managed to stutter, 'Again? You said again!' It seemed that Cole was about to repeat Walsh's verdict of 2005. It seemed that Alexandra's *X Factor* journey was once more coming to a premature end. 'Oh, my God, not again,' whispered Alexandra, almost unable to cope.

After a lengthy silence, Cole smiled and said, 'You're in my final three!'

It had been one of the most topsy-turvy verdicts delivered on the show. Cole had strongly hinted that she was not taking Alexandra any further. However, she was through. She collapsed on top of Cole and burst into floods of tears. When she emerged, she howled with joy and relief and shock.

Having composed herself at least enough to speak, she said, 'I'm looking forward to it! I can't wait! I'll work so hard! I swear to God I will.' Cole said she knew she would.

It was then time for Alexandra to rejoin O'Leary for her post-verdict chat. He was delighted for her. 'You finally did it, you finally did it,' he said.

Alexandra was in such a state of shock that she only managed to say, 'Just... oh, Dermot, thank you!'

It was time to ring home and deliver the good news. As she told her mother, who had performed at the highest level of music herself, Alexandra was full of pride and excitement. Her mother was overcome too by those emotions. She screamed with joy down the phone to her daughter. Three years on, Alexandra had made it to where she wanted to be: the live finals. Her mother was overjoyed for her and, frankly, it is hard to imagine that many viewers had dry eyes at this point. She had finally made it to the live shows where she would perform in front of a studio audience and an audience of millions of television viewers. Now it was time for the public to judge Alexandra.

CHAPTER EIGHT

THE LIVE
SHOWS

The live shows are filmed at the Fountain Studios in Wembley, North London and, as a spokesman explains, they are proud of their *X Factor* association. 'We are adept at making big live shows here but one of the biggest, in terms of the size of the set and the facilities needed, is *The X Factor* and its complementary ITV2 show, *The Xtra Factor*,' he says. 'We also recorded *Friends* at the studios for the London wedding storyline, which was a massive undertaking, with crews working till all hours. One night the producers even ordered pizza for the entire audience, who were still there at two in the morning waiting for script revisions to be made!'

For Alexandra, it was just where she wanted to be. Although she had been eliminated from the competition before this stage in 2005, she held no grudge against Louis Walsh, the judge who had sent her home that week – but she was determined to show how far she had come since then.

As usual, *The X Factor* audience packed into the studios to watch the drama unfold, while millions tuned in from home. In week one of the live shows, Alexandra was the first of the girls category to perform. Presenter O'Leary smiled and said, 'Now we say hello to the gorgeous queen of Tyneside. Hello, Cheryl! First live show, how do you feel?'

Cole replied that she felt a bit sick, adding, 'The nervous energy kind of rubs off.' But she agreed with O'Leary who reminded her that she had a great category. 'Well, first up,' she told the camera, 'is someone to prove to Louis that three years ago he actually lost his mind. It's the *gorgeous*... Alexandra.'

Then came the VT that preceded every performance of Alexandra – and all of the contestants – throughout the finals. 'Being where I am right now in the final twelve is the biggest thing that has ever happened to me,' said Alexandra, as natural in front of the camera as ever. 'I have to keep pinching myself every now and then, and reminding myself, "Wow, look where you are."' She then turned to her home life. As footage was shown of her Islington flat, her voiceover explained, 'I live in North London with my mum, my auntie, my sister and my two brothers.' She then spelled out the financial situation her family was in.

'We don't really have a lot,' she said. 'I have to sing in restaurants to make ends meet but I want something more now. When I really, really think what this show could do to my life, I get terrified.'

Then attention transferred to her mentor Cole, who described the challenge ahead for Alexandra. Explaining that her act had sung ballads so far throughout the competition, the Geordie said, 'Tonight I want to give her an upbeat song. She'll have to sing and dance, which is going to be a big challenge.'

Footage was shown of Alexandra working hard with choreographer Brian Friedman. 'Dancing and singing together isn't something I'm used to,' she said. 'I'm frightened that, if either of them go wrong, I could fall flat on my face.'

Friedman said, 'She can do both but, if she doesn't get them right on stage together, the performance will be a flop.'

As this VT was being shown to the audience, Alexandra was making her final preparations backstage and she had been hit by nerves. Indeed, just ten minutes earlier she had needed reassurance from her mentor, such was the level of her anxiety. Now it was approaching 'showtime' for her, she stood backstage holding her microphone and preparing herself for the challenge to come. The VT rolled on, with her pre-recorded voice predicting exactly how she would be feeling. 'When I step out on to that stage,' she said, 'it will be the biggest moment of my life.'

Then Walsh appeared on the screen, saying, 'Alexandra has waited for three years for this. I want her to go out there and prove it was worth the wait.'

The final words of the VT went to the girl herself. 'This is all I have wanted,' she said. 'I cannot fail or all my dreams are over.'

As a series of shots of her flashed across the screen, her name boomed through the speakers. She then took to the stage and stood on a specially raised platform. Wearing a short glittery dress, with her hair smoothed back, she looked amazing. Could her performance match her appearance?

It could. She sang 'I Wanna Dance With Somebody' and performed brilliantly. After a slow introduction she really ripped into the performance as it sped up. As the FizzyPop blog commented, 'Alexandra looked and sounded stunning singing a ballad intro then dancing up to "I Wanna Dance With Somebody".'

There were smiles all round from the judges as the audience heartily cheered and applauded Alexandra's performance. Cole, too, joined in the applause, holding her arms high as she clapped.

Louis Walsh tried to break through the noise to deliver his verdict. 'Alexandra!' he shouted. 'That was incredible! You look like a diva, you sing like a diva and you dance like a diva. I am so glad – you're amazing! Best performance of the night!'

Minogue went as far as to suggest that Alexandra had outperformed Whitney Houston. She said, 'Alexandra, I have to tell you I've seen Whitney perform that song and she just stood there and tapped on the microphone. You did all of that choreography incredibly. One thing that was missing, can you just look this way [points to Walsh] and go, "Agh!"'

Alexandra jokingly sneered at Walsh.

As the Irishman attempted to say that he had done Alexandra a favour, Minogue sighed and said, 'Oh, Lou – Lou!'

Cowell then interrupted and said, 'Hang on, Louis, enough, enough. Alexandra, it was a bit of an obvious song choice, you doing...' He was then interrupted himself by Cole who blew a raspberry of derision at him. 'You doing Whitney, I wouldn't have chosen the song. Having said that, I think you look fantastic. I think you managed to put your own interpretation on the song brilliantly. And now I am going to ask Louis Walsh to apologise to you.'

The audience were loving all this banter and cheered wildly.

'No! Alexandra! Did I do the right thing with you three years ago?' he pleaded with her.

Alexandra looked rather uncomfortable herself at

this point and said, 'You did because now I'm a better person now, I'm in a better state of mind.'

Cole then chipped in with, 'And you've got a better mentor!'

Alexandra agreed: 'I love Cheryl!'

Walsh then protested further, suggesting that he had actually done Alexandra a favour in 2005.

'I agree with that,' said Cowell.

It was time for Cole's comment. 'Alexandra, you owned that stage tonight. Considering how nervous you were ten minutes ago, you absolutely tore it up and I am so proud of you. I love you to bits.'

The judges' verdicts were positive – but what would the verdict of the voting public be? Throughout her two *X Factor* journeys, Alexandra had never faced a public vote. So she was nervous about the result.

At the end of the show, O'Leary announced the name of each act in turn that had been voted through. Alexandra cheered with relief and surprise when her name was announced. She had made it. The bottom two were the two girl bands Bad Lashes and Girlband. Bad Lashes were the act to be voted off and they left with the usual promise that we hadn't heard the last of them.

In week two it was the Michael Jackson theme that was chosen for the show. Alexandra was given the Jackson 5 song 'I'll Be There' to sing. Originally written by Berry Gordy Jr, Bob West, Hal Davis and

Willie Hutch, the song had been a hit not just for the Jacksons but also for Mariah Carey, who first sang it during an *MTV Unplugged* performance and later had a number-one hit with it. Carey's cover was to be the subject of debate when the judges came to give their verdicts after the performance.

Before any of that, though, we needed to see Alexandra's week-two VT, which was introduced by her mentor Cole. 'OK, first up, I don't really have to say much on this introduction: she's absolutely fantastic, it's the *beautiful* Alexandra Burke,' Cole said with a smile.

Her interview began with her discussing how she felt during the previous week's show. 'I waited for three years to step on that stage and to finally do it was phenomenal,' she said. 'To think that a couple of months ago I was singing in restaurants...'

Attention then turned to Cole, who once more discussed a very physical reaction to her act's performance. 'Alexandra last week looked incredible, sounded incredible and she gave me goose-bumps,' said the judge.

Next up was some home-movie footage of Burke and her siblings dancing and singing as youngsters. 'At the age of five I used to tell my mum, "Mum, I'm going to sing, I'm going to dance,"' said Burke's voiceover. 'They used to round up my brothers and sisters, and we used to sing, rap and record little videos.' She was seen rapping into the camera, saying 'Alexandra is here, wipe away your tears.'

All of this was great fun but then discussion turned to a more serious matter. 'This week, it feels like my voice is going,' said Alexandra, over footage of her sitting on some stairs looking disconsolate.

Scottish vocal coach Yvie Burnett was shown telling her not to sing, apart from in the dress rehearsal. 'Alexandra's voice is amazing. When she gets overexcited she uses her throat and forces her voice. And then the next day she loses her voice.'

Alexandra did well to listen to Burnett, who is the main vocal coach on both *The X Factor* and *Britain's Got Talent*, and has coached the likes of Shayne Ward and Leona Lewis to victory and beyond. As Louis Walsh put it, 'There are vocal coaches and there is Yvie Burnett; she is simply the best!'

She believes in the Estill Method, which is based on understanding how the vocal mechanism works. 'Yvie made me believe I could sing and actually made me enjoy it, which is half the battle,' said Lucy Benjamin, the winner of 2006's *X-Factor Battle Of The Stars*.

Burnett was not the only person giving Alexandra advice behind the scenes. The show's somewhat eccentric creative consultant Brian Friedman even went as far as advising her to write things down if she needed to chat with them, rather than saying them out loud. Alexandra complained that this made her appear diva-ish but Friedman was having none of it. 'If she loses her voice at week two, how is she even going to make it through further in this competition?' he asked.

Alexandra showed the camera a pad of paper on which she had written the word 'Help!'

But Cole agreed that her act had to keep quiet to preserve her asset. 'Alexandra has really had to rest her voice this week. Fingers crossed everything goes well on the night,' she concluded.

Then Alexandra was shown nervously telling the camera, 'I have given up so much to basically be here in this competition and I'm hoping that my voice doesn't give up on me.'

It was time to find out whether all the work – and rest – would prove worthwhile. As the audience applauded the evening's opening act, Alexandra appeared wearing a purple dress with her hair brushed over her left shoulder. She stood on the raised platform behind the judges and began to sing 'I'll Be There'. As she progressed through the first verse, she walked along the raised stage, towards the main stage. She was being supported by four backing singers, two male, two female, the females also in purple dresses. Alexandra joined them on the main stage, where she stood centrally, resting her microphone on the stand for the remainder of the song. Towards the end she began to really give the performance some soul, and made frantic arm movements. A starry white light illuminated her from behind and she looked like a megastar. It had been a magnificent performance and the audience gave her a standing ovation for it. Her mentor Cole applauded passionately and proudly.

But would the judges reflect the audience's passion in their comments? Once again, Walsh had to try to break through the noise in order to deliver the first verdict. 'Alexandra! A fantastic opening to the show,' he enthused. 'Last week you did Whitney, tonight you're doing Michael Jackson. You are world class, I love you and I can't believe that somebody with your talent is so humble. You've got it all going on, girl.' It seemed that Walsh was keen to make up for his previous rejection of Alexandra, as his endorsement was delivered with true passion and, within a matter of minutes, he would defend her from Cowell.

First, though, came Minogue, who smiled and said, 'It was definitely worth the wait. It was a faultless performance and I think it definitely propels this show into international standing. Thank you.' Praise indeed.

Alexandra at this point was clearly emotional, with tears in her eyes. Once more the audience and judges seemed to be united in respect for her. However, Cowell was about to balance all this positivity. 'Erm... OK, I'm going to start with a negative,' he said, to pantomime boos from the audience. 'Whitney last week, Mariah this week: it's all a bit predictable.'

The rest of the panel then protested that it was a Jackson 5 song that Alexandra had sung, not a Mariah Carey song. Walsh was particularly forceful in his heckling of Cowell.

'Mariah did this version,' retorted Cowell.

Alexandra managed a smile.

'The only reason I say that is that at the moment it's all a little bit copycat,' continued Cowell to further protests from Walsh. 'A little bit. The first half of the song was good, the second half of the song I have to tell you, though, was fantastic. But I think that what you've got to work out with Cheryl next week is that you've got to make you original. At the moment it's not, I've heard this before.'

Walsh countered that Cowell had not heard the same thing sung as well before.

It was time for Cole to step into the fray. 'Can I just say, for a start, it's not Mariah Carey week, it's Michael Jackson week, in case you didn't read the thing,' she said to huge support from the audience. 'That was a Michael Jackson song,' she repeated, clearly ruffled. 'And by the way, I wish someone would have told me when it was safe to sing Whitney or Mariah, because I'd have tried it meself. It's not a safe thing to do. It's a big song and you sang it amazingly. We're not playing Russian roulette here,

Simon, I'm not playing "can I get her out of the competition". I'm keeping her in and with that performance you are staying in the competition.'

Cowell told her she was being 'tetchy'.

O'Leary joined Alexandra centre-stage and asked Cowell, 'Are you just being picky for the sake of it tonight?'

'No,' he insisted. 'I just said to Cheryl, I actually did give you a compliment there. I was just trying to give you some constructive advice.' But this was the first serious disagreement of the series between Cowell and his new judge.

O'Leary alluded to the worries over her voice during the week and asked Alexandra how she felt. 'I'm feeling OK,' she replied. 'Yeah, I feel good.

O'Leary told her, 'You sounded great, honey.'

Indeed she did.

The bottom two that week were Ruth Lorenzo and Girlband. The two acts did the sing-off and then it came down to the judges to decide between the two. Walsh told both acts that they sang their hearts out. 'They gave everything but I'm looking after my first act... I am going to be loyal to my own act and the act that I have to send home is Ruth Lorenzo.'

Minogue said she hated deciding but also supported her own act Ruth, so voted for Girlband.

Cole said, 'Based on the last performance,

Ruth absolutely nailed it so I'll have to send home Girlband.'

The casting vote went to Cowell. 'Ruth, once again, unfortunately, you didn't play to your strengths. Girls, I think you've been given a really bad job by your mentor. It's not a question of what Louis has done for you, but hasn't done for you.' He took it to deadlock, which meant that the public vote would decide which of the two acts went home.

'The act that received the fewest votes and will be going home tonight is... Girlband. I'm sorry, girls. Congratulations, Ruth, well done.'

To be fair, their performance of 'Heal The World' had been far from ideal, so it was goodbye to them but onwards and upwards for Alexandra.

Onwards to week three, in fact, where Alexandra was the sixth act to perform on the night. Cheryl Cole, wearing a raunchy pink dress, introduced her as usual. 'OK, up next, prepare to have a little bit of fun with my gorgeous Alexandra Burke.'

The VT this week showed a less upbeat Alexandra than in previous rounds. It seemed that Cowell's feedback the previous week – although essentially positive – had hit a nerve with Burke. She said, 'Every time I perform I really, honestly try and give my own interpretation to the song.' The video then showed Cowell telling her the previous week that she was being too copycat and too predictable.

Cole then appeared and said, 'I don't care what Simon says about it was safe, it was obvious. It was a tough song to sing and she was amazing.' Cole was proving herself to be a fine mentor, with a wonderful protective streak. All the same, she could only protect her acts to a limited extent. The criticisms still had the potential to hurt them, as Alexandra showed in the video.

Footage was shown of her crying backstage after Cowell's comments in week two. She said, 'When I hear Simon say Diana's different, Laura's different but there's nothing special about me, it really upsets me.'

It was time for the video to take a happier turn, provided by her siblings Sheneice, Aaron and David. Aaron said of her week-two performance, 'Watching Alexandra sing onstage was just... amazing. She just looks like a total superstar and everyone at school is saying it.'

Sheneice then added, 'I just had to keep pinching myself and saying, "Oh, my God, that's my baby sister."'

Melissa, Alexandra's mum, then appeared, clearly full of pride. 'When I watch Alex on TV I am proud,' she said. 'It's a special gift and only very few people get it.'

Although these warm words of support were welcome, there was no hiding how hurt she had been by Cowell. It could perhaps be argued that Alexandra had got the matter out of proportion. Admittedly, in the cauldron of the competition, it would be easy to be oversensitive, but, all the same, Cowell had only offered mild criticisms amid fulsome praise. Had Alexandra overblown the issue? Cole might have believed this, as she said, 'Alexandra has got herself into a real state about Simon's comments.' Perhaps she was hinting that Alexandra needed some perspective.

'He's comparing me to my favourite artists and that's amazing,' explained Alexandra. 'I want Simon to have one week where he calls me an individual.'

The man himself was then shown. 'This is a huge song and, if she gets this right, she could absolutely tear the place apart,' he said.

Cole offered some support to her act and declared her faith in her. 'Alexandra needs to realise how amazing she's been so far. She's a strong woman and she can totally pull it off.'

The video ended with Alexandra offering some conclusive fighting talk. 'I'm here trying to fight for my career,' she said with steel. 'I'm not afraid to admit that I want to win any more.'

She was about to put on a winning performance and the song she had chosen was 'Candyman'. This raunchy big-band number had been a big hit for Christine Aguilera in 2007, earning her a Grammy award nomination for Best Female Vocal Pop

Performance. Musically, it is similar to the classic 'Boogie Woogie Bugle Boy' but includes some rather steamy lyrics. Alexandra later admitted that she had reservations singing about how the man made her 'panties drop' and her 'cherry drop' in front of her relatives. 'I first refused to sing it,' she says. 'It's too sexy! When I had a rehearsal with it, Simon said, "You do understand this is going to turn you around?" From there it just sort of picked up. I thought, I just have to have fun and let my hair down. If you want to do sex appeal, do sex appeal. Just start letting your hair down a bit more.'

Indeed, when it came to the live show it was all right on the night. Dressed up in a camp naval outfit and flanked by male and female dancers and backing vocalists dressed in sailor outfits, she positively nailed the song. The male dancers added to the spectacle, even flirting with Walsh at one point. Alexandra was breathless at the conclusion and held her hands in a praying position as she waited for the judges to have their say.

'Alexandra,' started Walsh, 'what a total transformation! You're not the same girl from the past two weeks. I loved everything about it. I loved the styling, the dancing, the choreography. You're back in this race and you deserve to be in the race.'

The audience howled their approval for Walsh's praise.

Minogue essentially just echoed her fellow judge. Pointing at the Irishman, she said, 'Ditto to everything you said!' She then turned to Alexandra and said, 'Candyman? Sweeeeet! You're back. You look amazing.'

Now came the moment Alexandra had waited for all week – Simon Cowell's comments. Would she get the praise she so craved from the straight-talking judge? 'Alexandra, when I watched the film back, maybe it has seemed a little bit unfair,' he began. 'The only reason I said what I said is that, not only do I like you as a singer, I like you as a person. Backstage I know how worried you've been. All I've been waiting for is the performance that shows us that you are potentially a great artist, and you just delivered it.'

This came as a huge relief to Alexandra. True, there was the small matter of the public vote yet to be resolved. However, assuming that she passed through that, she could spend the week bolstered by positive comments from the judges, including Simon. She exhaled with relief and then shrieked, 'Thank you, Simon! Wooo!' The pressure lifting off her shoulders was palpable.

Cowell was not finished though. 'And that is a tough song to sing,' he said, wagging his finger at Alexandra. 'That is not an easy song to sing with everything going on around you. But it was a fantastic performance and that's what I loved about it.'

Once more, Alexandra thanked him. Then it was time for her mentor Cole to offer her own supportive feedback. 'First of all, I'd like to say to Louis that she was never out of the running, thank you very much. Second of all, Alexandra, what I wanted to show tonight is that cheeky personality we know you've got, like Simon said backstage. And you proved your individuality and that you're an all-rounder. You can do the lot and that was amazing.'

Alexandra was overjoyed with the feedback. This had been a big week for her, moving away from the comfort zone of ballads to perform an up-tempo song. As she had been told more than once, to really make it big and prove that she had the x factor, Alexandra had to show she could perform a range of styles. A winning voice was only half of the battle – she needed to have more. Having proved that she did indeed have more, and having that acknowledged by the panel, was a big moment for her. 'Thank you, Cheryl, thank you, guys!' she said, beaming.

When O'Leary rejoined Alexandra, he said, 'It's a big camp armada. Are you sure you're not in Louis's category?'

This harmless quip would lead to further banter the following week, and banter that would ignite some controversy. But, for now, O'Leary simply asked Alexandra how she had felt performing 'Candyman'. 'I found it really fun and I'm very thankful for this song, so thank you to Cheryl and Simon for making me realise that this was a good song choice,' Alexandra said, smiling.

The first act confirmed as through was Eoghan. He bent down, punched the air and shouted, 'Yes!' Alexandra was the next act announced and she jumped up and down in celebration. First she hugged Cheryl, then Laura and then Diana. It came down to a bottom two of Daniel Evans and Scott Bruton. Both acts performed again and then the judges voted for which of them would be sent home. It came down to a casting vote for Walsh. The Irishman had been very harsh towards Evans for several weeks, so it was expected that he would send him home. He said, 'It's not always easy being a judge on this show and this is one of those times. I think the public got it absolutely right though. It was the highest standard. In the sing-off, one person went through the motions and one person sang every word like he meant it, so I'm going to have to send home Scott.' Walsh became quite emotional at this point and Bruton, who had been voted off the show as a result of Walsh's decision, was rather petulant in defeat.

However, Alexandra was joyful in her victory as she moved through to fight another week.

The following week saw a disco theme on *The X Factor*. This has traditionally been a week that separates the wheat from the chaff on reality pop shows. Not only does the theme inherently show up those acts for whom dancing is a problem, but also disco songs are deceptively difficult to sing. Therefore, many of the acts were nervous on the evening. A criticism offered by Walsh to some of the early acts was that there was no dancing involved. He told Diana Vickers, in particular, 'I'd have liked to see you dancing a little bit.'

So when Cole introduced Alexandra, she promised some fine moves. 'Louis wants dancing? Here we go, it's Alexandra Burke,' said the Geordie proudly.

It was time for Alexandra's VT of the week and this time round it would be a far happier affair. It kicked off with Alexandra saying, 'Saturday night was the best performance ever in my life. It was amazing to see everyone off their seats. Cheryl was enjoying it.'

Cole herself then chipped in, smiling proudly and saying, 'She absolutely blew everyone away.'

Alexandra's upbeat mood was not just due to her performance the previous week. During the week, she had been to the premiere of the new James Bond film and she had also been shipped some home cooking to cheer her up. Twice during the week her mother drove from Islington to the contestants' Wembley home to give her some Caribbean soul food. 'Alex is fine but she misses her mum's home cooking,' Bell told a local newspaper. 'She needed something to keep her spirits up, so I did spicy Jamaican chicken, peas, homemade macaroni cheese, coleslaw and a nice crisp green salad.' Home food is always a winner to comfort a homesick offspring, as Bell confirmed. 'She's having a great time and she's keeping well. On Wednesday she attended the James Bond film premiere with the other contestants. Mum's food will give her strength. She'll need everything she's got because it's disco week Saturday. I think she'll really excel herself.'

It was not just her proud mother who had high hopes that Alexandra would excel. Another boost came her way when Manchester United and England football star Wayne Rooney predicted she would win, as revealed by Rooney's wife Coleen McLoughlin, who also explained that a nod from her husband was a positive thing to receive. 'We love watching the show and [Wayne] picked out Leona two years ago from watching her very first audition. Then he tipped Leon to beat Rhydian in the final,' said McLoughlin. 'I wouldn't have a clue who is going to win this year. Cheryl has the strongest group but it's who the public likes. I like Laura and Diana but Wayne is confident it's Alex.' This unexpected nod from Rooney was a great boost to Alexandra's spirits as she prepared for disco week.

So it was no wonder Alexandra was buzzing on her VT, where she said, 'This week for me has been the most special week out of the whole competition. A couple of weeks ago I was working in a restaurant and now people are coming up saying, "Alex! Can we take a picture?" "Yeah, sure!" The premiere was just unbelievable! I was on the red carpet. I remember turning round and seeing Judi Dench and thinking, I have to give this woman a kiss! I've finally been given a taste of what my life could be like in years to come.'

But it was then on to business and Cole explained that she thought the song she had chosen was one of the best disco songs of all time.

'I'm really excited about my song this week,' said Alexandra. 'I've got four male dancers. They are hot – oh, my God!'

Cole smiled and said that Alexandra had to 'stay focused and remember it's about her vocals'.

Pop Idol winner Will Young had been coaching the contestants that week and he had some constructive criticisms for her. 'I think Alexandra can belt her voice too much. I noticed she was getting a bit raspy,' he said. He was then shown at the rehearsals saying, 'You know, just start off at about seventy per cent.'

Alexandra appeared in no way defensive about these comments from a young man who knew – after all – what it took to win a show such as this. Quite the opposite, in fact: 'It's exciting for me because I want to know what I'm doing wrong,' she said.

Young concluded, 'She really has to have lots of lessons and make sure she doesn't lose that voice.'

Once more, she was being advised to not lose her voice. Alexandra doesn't just like to sing, she likes to chat too. Left, right and centre, she was being told to rest her voice from time to time. For the bubbly Burke, this was easier said than done!

Again, she concluded her VT with fighting talk. 'Every week you have to get better and better to survive,' she said. 'I really wanna make it to the end of this competition.' And it was time for the talking to stop and the singing to begin as she once more took to the stage.

The song she had chosen to sing this week was Donna Summer's classic 'On The Radio'. Released in 1979, this track was her tenth top-ten hit. It has since been covered by Emmylou Harris, Selena and Martine McCutcheon. Significantly, it was the song chosen by Michelle McManus in the second series of *Pop Idol*, and she went on to win the series. Alexandra's performance began with her sitting on a chaise longue in the middle of a stage swept with dry ice. Wearing a shiny short silver dress and a remembrance poppy, she stood up and danced after the intro, accompanied by the aforementioned four dancers, who were all topless. She toyed with them, flicking one over midway through the song. During the performance she showed what a great mover she was, combining winning vocals with some cool dancing.

The audience had loved every minute of

Alexandra's bopping performance, and almost lifted the roof off the studio with appreciation. Louis Walsh shouted through the acclaim to speak to Alexandra. He said, 'Alexandra, last week – amazing. Tonight, you picked a Donna Summer song and very few girls can sing a Donna Summer song. You did, you sang, you danced, you performed. I loved Brian Friedman's choreography, I loved the outfit, I loved everything.'

Amid the applause that greeted Walsh's feedback, Cowell could be heard to say, 'I bet you did,' in reference to his fellow judge's approval of the dancers.

The Irishman bit back, meowing at Cowell, 'Actually, you're still wearing the platforms, Simon, from the disco era.'

This was to be far from the end of the row, as we shall see.

Meanwhile, Minogue had yet to give her verdict on Alexandra's performance. 'You know, Alexandra, the big, big stars of the music industry today are the ones who can tour and do all of that,' she said. 'Every week you show us it would be the most amazing concert to come and see you. That was great.'

Alexandra gleefully thanked the judge.

It was time for Cowell to comment. 'Alexandra, I've got to tell you you're the most improved performer,' he said. 'Something has now clicked with you. You've got your confidence back.' Turning to

Walsh, Cowell said, 'Still now it takes me back that you didn't put her in three years ago.'

As mass laughter and applause erupted, Alexandra could be heard to say, 'Oh, God.'

Walsh, meanwhile, was quick to stand up for himself. 'Simon, Simon,' he pleaded. 'Excuse me, may I explain? That year, I picked Shayne Ward and he won the final. So I did her a favour.'

Cowell was not about to give up without a fight. 'He's not a girl,' he said back.

Walsh and Cowell do banter very well, and the Irishman countered, 'He won the show by the way, in case you didn't know,' said Walsh. 'His name is Shayne. I did her a favour, I did her a favour, Simon.'

Alexandra, meanwhile, said, 'I love you, Shayne!'

Cowell then bit back at Walsh. 'Louis, I don't know what time of the month it is for you but just calm it down,' he sneered. There was an eruption of laughter and Alexandra, too, seemed to be loving the verbal battle. Cowell turned the conversation back to her. 'Alexandra, back to you, it was once again a great, great performance,' he said. 'Congratulations.'

Cole had enjoyed the Cowell/Walsh clash but was also overjoyed at how well her act was developing. It was a source of great pride for her that she had chosen Alexandra at the judges'-houses stage. Week after week, in the live shows, her decision was being vindicated. 'You said in your VT you have to get stronger and stronger every week to stay in this competition,' she told her act. 'That's exactly what you do, Alexandra. I'm always so proud of you, you never put me down and what's clicked is you're starting to believe it and starting to enjoy it now, and that's what we all want to see. Well done.'

O'Leary then stepped back on to the stage to wrap up Alexandra's slot as normal – only this week things were going to be rather abnormal. 'From a layman's point of view I don't think it was camp enough,' he said. 'And Louis, I'm *sure* you liked Brian's choreography there,' he said. Walsh looked aggrieved. O'Leary then turned to Alexandra and said, 'Do you agree with what Simon said there, do you think something has clicked in the last few weeks? Do you feel more confident?'

The weight lifting off her shoulders was visible. 'To be honest with you, after last week, because I didn't care about vocal for once,' said Alexandra with a sigh, 'I just smiled and I had fun; that's the first time I've ever really enjoyed myself performing. Because of last week it's made me much stronger to come on stage and not care – just smile and enjoy it. I don't know how long it's going to last, I just have to enjoy it.'

That was the end of the night performance-wise for Alexandra but a storm was brewing in the studio. O'Leary's banter with Walsh about the topless dancers during Alexandra's act might have seemed harmless enough to viewers. Indeed, Cowell has made many similar jokes during the history of *The X Factor*, as did Sharon Osbourne during her reign on the show. Even during the show in question, Cowell had joked to Walsh, 'I bet you [enjoyed the choreography].' However, it seemed Walsh was fuming when O'Leary entered the fray and it was not the first time in the evening that O'Leary had joked this way.

When Walsh had criticised the male angel dancers who had danced alongside Rachel Hylton, the presenter quipped, 'Wow, I never thought I'd hear Louis Walsh say that hunky angels were average.' But there was a serious question. Would Alexandra also be moving on to another week when the results came in? O'Leary announced the seven contestants who would make it through, leaving the bottom two to sing again.

The first through was Daniel Evans. 'You're kidding me!' said Evans in shock and sank to his knees. The second act named was Alexandra, who seemed less shocked by this than in previous weeks and, as she hugged her fellow contestants and mentor Cole, Simon Cowell could be seen looking at her with pride and approval. Although not in his category, Alexandra had clearly caught Cowell's imagination with her talent.

This week's bottom two were Austin Drage and Rachel Hylton, both forced to sing again in the showdown. Minogue admitted that her act, Hylton, had made mistakes earlier in the night and Cowell told both acts they had to fight for their place. Hylton fought that bit harder and survived the judges' verdicts to fight another week, while Drage's *X Factor* journey was over. But Austin's mentor Simon Cowell said, 'We haven't seen the last of him.'

Walsh, who cast the deciding vote, said, 'I'm going to save who I think is a raw talent.' The Irishman also claimed that Drage had not connected with his audience.

Drage bit back at Walsh in the days following his exit. 'To be honest with you, I thought that was a bit of a silly thing to say, because obviously I've connected with the audience every week since starting the competition,' he said. 'I've connected with the audience as much as anybody else but I haven't had the great songs that everybody else had, I haven't been that lucky.' Asked who he thought would win, Drage replied, 'Laura White because she's really talented and she's a musician, and that's what I want to see more of – more musicians playing music, and not puppets. I wish her all the best of luck.'

He had been one of the favourites early on, proving that this year's *X Factor* was both tough and hard to call. Alexandra watched Drage leave with some shock, and became ever more determined to up her game and work hard. She wanted to go all the way to the top and would do whatever it took to get there.

Alexandra had her first taste of the top when the single recorded by *The X Factor* finalists went to number one. The song they had chosen to record was Mariah Carey's hit 'Hero', in aid of a very special cause, with the proceeds split between the Poppy Appeal and Help For Heroes. Described by Prime Minister Gordon Brown as a 'national institution', Help For Heroes gives assistance to British soldiers who have been injured during their service. Since its launch in October 2007, it has raised £1 million a month to help support wounded servicemen and women injured in the current conflicts. Even before *The X Factor* involvement, the organisation had enjoyed celebrity backing. Footballing royalty David Beckham said, 'I'm incredibly proud and grateful for the commitment and work that our armed forces do for the country. I support the campaign fully.'

Other famous supporters include Prince Harry, broadcaster Jeremy Clarkson... and Simon Cowell. In fact, it was Cowell who agreed to link *The X Factor* with Help For Heroes by getting the finalists to record a fundraising single. 'It's too good an opportunity to pass up,' said Cowell. 'It is a great way to pay something back to the men and women who give so much for this country. And it shows what music can do – it shows it can be a force for good. Quite frankly, I was appalled that these guys risk their lives every day for us and don't get much in return. They are our unsung heroes and I am honoured to be working for them and alongside them. I want to stress that all the proceeds from this single will go to this brilliant cause. It's going to be amazing. I don't expect many dry eyes in the studio when they hear it for the first time. This song will go straight to the top of the charts.'

Scott Bruton, mentored by Cowell in the boys category, agreed, saying, 'It's brilliant to be able to put the single out and hopefully raise a lot of money for a very important cause.'

Alexandra and her fellow finalists recorded the single at the famous Metropolis Studios in West London. Many iconic recordings have been made there, including The Verve's classic album *Urban Hymns*, The Stone Roses' controversial *The Second Coming*, and Queen's *Made In Heaven* and *Innuendo* albums. For Alexandra, to be in this studio was a joy. Not that she was entirely new to recording studios but Metropolis was special. 'I have been in studios before but not like this one,' she said. 'We can't wait to hear the song on the radio and it feels so good to know that we are in a position to help.'

Everyone involved was excited about the venture.

The British Army Chief General Sir Richard Dannatt said of the charity, 'I very much welcome the work Help For Heroes has done to generate extra support for the Armed Forces and to raise money to further improve the care our troops receive when injured. I urge you to back this wonderful campaign. The Armed Forces genuinely appreciate your support.'

The single was made available to download immediately after its Saturday-night television debut on 25 October. It was released in the shops two days later – at the start of the two-week run up to Remembrance Sunday. Bryn Parry, co-founder of Help For Heroes said, 'This is a wonderful initiative by X Factor and we hope that the whole country will get behind the single. It would be fantastic if it became a hit and I would like to think that it will become the anthem for our Heroes, the extraordinary men and women who are injured while serving our country. Please get out there and buy this single and show you care; thank you.'

The acts showed how much they cared by visiting the forces rehab centre Headley Court near Leatherhead in Surrey, where war heroes are battling to overcome appalling war wounds. Alexandra was deeply moved by this visit and what she saw there. Drying tears from her eyes, she said of the patients, 'To see them so smiley and happy has been really emotional. It was hard not to cry in front of them.

Honestly, this has been the most humbling experience of my life.'

Lance Corporal Terry Byrne told Spanish hopeful Ruth Lorenzo how much their trip meant to the injured soldiers and marines. Paratrooper Terry, 24, lost his lower right leg to a Taliban-laid landmine in the Afghan badlands two months ago. The modest NCO, with 2 Para in Colchester, Essex, told her, 'It's really great that you're showing an interest in what happens to us. It's a great morale boost to see you down here.'

Hugging the injured trooper, Lorenzo replied, 'You guys are the nation's heroes. We're just on TV. That's nothing compared to what you have done.'

Meanwhile, another Afghan hero, Lance Bombardier Ben Parkinson, tapped out a message to boy band JLS on his keyboard. Parkinson astounded doctors after surviving a blast in Helmand Province two years ago. He lost both legs, suffered multiple fractures to his skull, jaw, spine and elbow, and his voicebox was shattered. Ben and his family have led a long campaign to boost paltry compensation payouts offered to soldiers like him who have been crippled for life in Afghanistan and Iraq. JLS star Marvin Humes, 23, said, 'What is so amazing about meeting Ben and all the other blokes here is what strong characters they are. He was even cracking jokes with us over his machine. His determination to recover is incredible – and there is not a single ounce of self-pity about him.'

Band-mate Ortise Williams, 21, added, 'I've read about Ben in the paper, so it's an honour to meet him.'

As Alexandra's fellow category member Diana Vickers gently stroked paralysed Rifleman Stephen Vause's hand, her eyes began to well up. Stephen, 20, sustained terrible head injuries when an insurgent mortar round exploded in Basra. Vickers said, 'He makes you realise all your little worries are nothing. Stephen can't speak and has little movement – and all because he was fighting out there for us. I'm just so pleased we can try to give something back to him now with the single.'

They did indeed give something back – the single went straight to number one, and sold 313,244 copies in its first week of release – outselling the entire top 10 combined. Among those who bought it was Prime Minister Gordon Brown. So it was that Alexandra had her first number-one hit. It would not be the last.

CHAPTER NINE

'YOU MAKE ME PROUD TO BE BRITISH'

In week five, Alexandra faced the long wait to perform as the final act of the night. Alexandra watched seven acts perform before her, then it was time for her mentor Cheryl Cole to introduce her. 'Last but certainly not least, it's the gorgeous Alexandra Burke,' she said.

Once more, via her VT, we got a glimpse of her week. 'Last week I got on stage and shook what my mumma gave me and absolutely loved it. I think it had something to do with them boys!'

Cole added, 'Alexandra has had an amazing past couple of weeks. This girl is on fire.'

We then saw Alexandra ringing home to tell her family that the finalists had made it to number one with their 'Hero' single. 'I used to listen to the charts with my brothers and sisters in my living room and now... Oh, my gosh – we're number one. The fact that the single is for such a great cause, it makes it even better.'

Alexandra had met the legendary diva Mariah Carey during the week, which she described in her VT. 'Meeting Mariah Carey was indescribable,' she said, smiling. 'I've dreamed of this moment since I was a little girl.'

Cole then told viewers, 'I have chosen the best, most classic, most beautiful Mariah song for Alexandra.'

However, this song choice brought a sense of pressure to Alexandra. 'I feel like I'm under a lot of pressure this week because I just feel like it's a big song and it's a lot to live up to.' Recalling with a giggle the rehearsals, she said, 'When I was singing I couldn't even look at her, I was looking down to the floor. So I realise my emotions got the better of me.' Footage was then shown of her apologising to Carey. 'Sorry about that second chorus, I didn't realise where I was going there,' says Alexandra sheepishly.

Carey was gracious in response: 'No, we're rehearsing – rehearsal! It sounded beautiful though.' During a piece to camera, Carey said, 'I really liked Alexandra. I felt by the end we were like old friends.'

Alexandra later returned the compliment, saying, 'She's not a diva. No way. She'd say hello to us in the corridors backstage.'

But later in the series, another famous American female singer would be less friendly backstage.

The VT then returned to Alexandra's rehearsal where, having been reassured by Carey, she said, 'I'm not nervous any more!'

The diva was pleased, telling the contestant, 'See! We're just friends now.' Alexandra had truly loved meeting Carey and said, 'I never thought I'd get that chance to meet her. It made me realise that dreams can come true.'

The other judges then appeared to add a bit of edge to the VT. Cowell said, 'This is the week that will simply make her or break her.'

Meanwhile, Walsh sniffed, 'Anything less than perfect will be a failure for Alexandra.'

Naturally, Cole was supportive of her girl and dismissive of the other judges' games. 'I'm actually past caring what the others say about Alexandra. She's going to come out and she's going to knock them dead.'

Alexandra herself, though, was less confident, spelling it out at the close of her VT. 'Everyone is saying, "This is your week, this is your week." But I. Am. Terrified.'

Would she knock them dead as Cole predicted? Or would her nerves get the better of her performance? It was time to find out.

Alexandra appeared in a spangly light-brown dress

and performed with a backing choir that was dressed in black. Heidi Stephens, in her hilarious live blog on the *Guardian* website, said of Alexandra's performance, 'Oh Lord, she's singing "Without You" – originally a hit for Nilsson, later murdered by Mariah, hopefully now redeemed by Alexandra. It's a bloody miserable song but she's doing a cracking job. Can she hit the big note? YES, SHE CAN. Forget JLS, let's vote Alexandra in. Performance of the night, in my humble opinion.'

And the reception from the audience was unprecedented. The applause and cheering continued throughout Walsh's comments and well into Minogue's feedback. Walsh fought to speak over the cheers and said, 'Alexandra, you're getting better week after week after week. That was the biggest vocal challenge of the night and you won it. I'm hearing little bits of Whitney, Mariah, Toni Braxton. Alexandra, that was the best performance of the night by far.'

Minogue, too, was mighty pleased. 'An absolute standout performance,' she said. 'You look beautiful but what I also love to see is the funny side of you; when you came back after meeting Mariah it was like a little kid in a playground, you were so excited. All of that emotion is real, I know it's been a great week for you.'

Simon Cowell might have made a small factual

mistake in his verdict but he was still very positive. 'I love your attitude, your enthusiasm. The fact that you're loving it. We don't hear you whining and complaining. Let's be honest, anyone who gets the chance to perform in front of 12 million people – you're in a great performance. I have to say, you're 19 years old...'

Alexandra chipped in to remind him she was '20 now, 20 now'.

'All right, whatever.' Cowell smiled. 'You're singing one of the big Mariah classics, she's like ten feet away and that, by any standards, was outstandingly good.'

Cole then spoke and said that she felt Alexandra's nerves prior to the big performance. 'Do you know what? I know how terrified you were. But as Mariah said, you're one of the very few people who are able to use those nerves in a positive way. That for me was your best performance throughout the whole series.'

Praise from all the panel then, including another glowing report from Cowell, which always meant so much to Alexandra.

O'Leary then joined Alexandra centre-stage and asked her how much it had meant for her to meet and work with her childhood heroine Mariah Carey. 'I cried like six times when I met her. The moment I saw her foot coming down the stairs I was in tears. She is an inspiration to me and lots of other people. I'd probably be the same if I met Whitney or Aretha but she's just a star and I fulfilled one dream by meeting her, so I'm thankful. Thanks to my family too. I love you guys!'

The public loved Alexandra too. They once more voted her through comfortably to fight another week. The results left a bottom two of Laura White and Ruth Lorenzo. The casting vote went to Walsh, after two judges voted to send Laura home and one voted to send home Ruth. 'Dermot, it just goes to show the high standard this year, it's an incredible standard. That sing-off was just unbelievable, I loved both songs. But I have to vote somebody off and it's a really difficult job to do. I love both girls. I thought they were incredible tonight. I have to pick somebody so I'm going to pick the person with the most fight left in her, the most fight to stay in the competition. Dermot, the person I am sending home tonight – regrettably – is Laura.'

White stood in shock, while Lorenzo cried with a mixture of relief, shock and sadness. The audience loudly booed Walsh's decision and there was widespread shock.

'I was absolutely distraught by the end of the night. I feel like I've given my all and it's not happened for me this time,' said Laura. 'It was time for me to go. I look at everything as fair and I feel it was my time to go for whatever reason. Being in the bottom two was a horrific feeling. It was horrendous to sing for my life. It was tough to be told that I was not going to be saved and I had to go home. I'm really, really proud of myself. I watched it back and I didn't see how it was one of my weakest. I think I've learned a lot about myself. I believe in myself a lot more than I did. I started off in this competition just to meet Simon and sing to Simon, and I ended up in the live shows.'

The following week, O'Leary introduced Cole, saying she was 'fast becoming a national treasure'. Alexandra was not to be far behind. Her VT began with her saying, 'Saturday night was amazing. I really gave it some and a half. I saw the judges standing, I saw the audience standing, I literally felt like Beyoncé. It was great!!'

Again Cole was full of pride as she looked back at her act's great song: 'Alexandra's was the performance of the week last week. It just makes me so proud of her.'

Footage was then shown of Alexandra visiting her North London home. 'We all got to go home this week, which was so important to me. [I] got to see my mum, my dad, my brothers and sisters – my whole family. People I've lived with for years are coming up to me and saying, "Come on, let's take a picture on my phone." It's like, "Uh, uh. I literally live next door to you, it's so weird!"'

Alexandra's sister Sheneice said, 'I miss her so much, I feel like I've lost my left arm.'

Alexandra had shared a bed with Sheneice and, as she returned to that bedroom, she said, 'Going back to my old room and to the bed I used to share with my sister was an uplifting experience because it showed me how much I really, really want to change everything around me.'

Back behind the scenes of the show, Alexandra was told by a vocal coach that her song for the week was 'about simplicity, it's not about showing off. I'm taking you right back, rather than making you belt all the time.'

Brian Friedman agreed that it was a song to hold back on.

Cowell chipped in, saying, 'There's no hiding on this song, it's totally and utterly about the voice.'

Once more, Alexandra concluded the VT on a slightly mixed note. Looking back to the previous week, she said, 'Laura going showed me that no one knows who's going to go next. I'm going to fight so hard to make sure it ain't me.'

What would her song for the night be? Written by Billy Preston and Bruce Fisher, 'You Are So Beautiful' was first made popular by Joe Cocker. It has since been covered by scores of artists including Bonnie Tyler, Diana Ross, Kenny Rogers and Westlife. She sang it beautifully and received particularly positive praise from Walsh, the man who had broken her dream three years earlier. He said, 'Alexandra, you are getting better week by week by week. You're so professional. You made that beautiful song, lots of emotion. What I want the public to know is that every time I see you in the corridors you are so happy, so professional. You never whinge, unlike some of the other people in this show. You totally deserve to be in this competition. I'm totally behind you. I want the public to get behind you because you're a rare raw talent.'

Minogue then said, 'Alexandra, you've heard it from me before; there's nothing you can't sing. What I loved about that is that you sang a song which is a male vocal song, giving you the chance to put your stamp on it. But I would like to see more of your personality come onstage because we do love you backstage so show us a little bit more. Those lyrics are happy lyrics – show it to us.'

However, it was Cowell who stole the show among the judges, jokingly asking Alexandra, 'You were singing that to me, weren't you?'

The contestant, ever up for a bit of fun, replied, 'Oh, most definitely! That was *so* for Simon!'

Cowell laughed along and said, 'Thank you, that meant a lot! I've got to say, Alexandra, that is honestly one of the most difficult songs to sing. As Danni says, it's tough when you sing a song that was originally sung by a guy. That's what I wanted to see you and hear you do this week. No frills, just being a good old-fashioned singer. Look, we have had a lot of controversy over the last week because a great singer did leave the competition. This show is all about finding a great new singer, that's why I'm really hoping you'll stay in the competition after that performance because it was terrific.'

Alexandra's mentor Cole sat smiling proudly and said, 'Wow, wow, wow. Other than the fact that each week you're growing into a little star and I genuinely believe you're going to have a huge career after this, I just absolutely love working with you, Alexandra, and I love you to pieces. That was amazing, thank you.'

Amazing indeed and more than enough to get her through to the next week. The bottom two were Daniel Evans and Rachel Hylton. Evans sang 'Bridge Over Troubled Water' and Hylton sang 'One Love' by Mary J Blige. The judges voted to send Evans home, so Hylton would be joining Alexandra in the following week's show.

A week in which Alexandra opened the show. 'First up tonight, she's hot and she's Alexandra Burke!' said Cole, ahead of the pre-performance VT.

'Last week I was there on that stage in my little baby-doll dress, had smoke surrounding me, singing this beautiful song and I literally felt like I'd died and gone to heaven,' said Alexandra.

Cole said, 'Once again, Alexandra delivered an

amazing performance, and each week I just get more and more proud of her.'

For Alexandra, *The X Factor* was confirming to her that singing was what she was born to do; *all* she wanted to do, in fact. 'This is all I ever see myself doing: singing and making people smile when I sing. This week I had a master-class with Gary and Mark from Take That. I used to have their picture frames on my wall, their bedsheets, their pillowcases, so I was a huge Take That fan.' She was shown rehearsing with Gary Barlow and Mark Owen, and told them, 'Oh, my gosh, I will be reading the words, I'm so sorry.'

They said not to worry and that they had to do that with their own songs too. They were clearly impressed, Barlow saying during a piece to camera, 'When I think of *The X Factor* I see Alexandra straight away. She's got the classic diva voice. We were blown away.'

However, a new concern had arisen over Alexandra. 'You have got an unbelievable voice and you should take care of it,' said Barlow, referring not only to how much she sang – but also to how much she talked!

'This is thing – I'm not [taking care of her voice],' said Alexandra.

'You really need to stop talking so much,' replied Barlow.

'Even Ruth told me...' began Alexandra.

Barlow interrupted, 'No, don't say anything else. Just stop it!'

Next up in the VT Alexandra explained that her performance would include a major dance routine, and fears were expressed that the dance moves would affect her voice. Remembering her encounter with Barlow, Alexandra laughed. 'He told me I talk too much and I have to agree with him!'

On the night her voice held out brilliantly. She sang 'Relight My Fire' and, according to many online wags, she outsang the Take That version. 'I thought that was better than the actual Take That version,' wrote *Guardian* blogger Jack Arnott. The judges, too, were massively impressed.

Walsh said, 'Alexandra Burke, you are what *The X Factor* is all about. You're young, you're talented. I love the way you didn't just copy the original. Alexandra, I think you're an incredible girl. What people at home don't know is that you've got an amazing personality backstage. I. Want. You. In. The Final.'

Next up to speak was Minogue. The Aussie said, 'Alexandra, brilliant performance. You didn't look as if you warmed up until halfway through. You look really nervous tonight. Is that because it's the first performance?'

There were audience boos at this point and Alexandra replied, 'I'm always nervous, I'm a nervous wreck. You know what? I just wanted to come out onstage and have fun for once! And I'm telling you, if I can come onstage and shake what my mum's given me then, boy, I'm happy!' So that was that slightly awkward moment very well negotiated by the contestant!

Cowell then commented, and once more stole the show. 'Again, I don't think you've had enough credit for what a great performer you are. Every time you're given a song you put on a show. You're 19, 20 years old. We don't have many singers in this country of this quality. I think...'

Walsh interrupted to say, 'Simon, can I say something? I think she's the best singer we've had since Leona. I really, really do.'

Cowell continued, 'Yeah but I just hope that people don't think that you're safe because I think you've got to make it through to the finals. Actually, that was one of the best versions of that song I've ever heard.'

The public did indeed give her enough votes to once more avoid the bottom two and the dreaded sing-off. The two acts there were Walsh's band JLS and Minogue's Rachel Hylton. After both acts had performed again, Walsh said, 'I totally believe in JLS so the act I am sending home is Rachel.'

Minogue: 'Fantastic performances tonight, we're at the pointy end of the competition. But hands down I have to say, Rachel, that was the performance. The act I have to send home is JLS.'

Cole: 'I wish I didn't have to do this. Guys, I loved what you did. I loved the little twist on the song there. Rachel, I thought that was the best you've sung since the auditions. This is a horrible thing to do but I'm going to have to send home Rachel.'

Cowell: 'This is tough. You know, Rachel, I've been a fan of yours ever since you first came on this show and I really like you. But it's been three times? JLS, I don't know what went wrong tonight. I don't think you should have been in the bottom two. That was a great choice of song by the way.'

Walsh attempted to turn up the heat on Cowell and encourage him to save his act. He said, 'You have to save JLS!'

Cowell coolly turned and said, 'I don't have to do anything.'

'Yes, you do,' protested Walsh.

Cowell repeated with extra emphasis, 'I don't have to do anything.'

After a lengthy pause, Cowell said, 'All right, the act I'm going to send home – and I really, really don't like saying this – is Rachel.'

Alexandra, meanwhile, sailed through to the next round when a very special visitor would be present in *The X Factor* studios.

If the presence of Carey and Take That had sent excitement in *X Factor* land ever higher, the arrival of Britney Spears the following week would see people almost freak out with joy. When news had spread that Britney was to perform on *The X Factor*, there was widespread excitement. It was to be her first visit to the United Kingdom since her tour more than four years previously, so this was quite a coup for the show. A source from *X Factor* told the *Sun*, 'Everyone is thrilled. To have Britney involved is a massive coup. They expect ratings to go through the roof when her performance airs.'

X Factor boss and judge Cowell himself agreed: 'I'm really excited about it because she's got her act together now and the new record's terrific. She's come back from a very dark place and is a great artist. I think that what's happened in the last two years has made her more interesting. She wants to be the biggest star in the world again – and she's got a shot.'

Alexandra, too, wanted to the biggest star in the world one day, but first she would have to negotiate another week on *The X Factor*, which had been given an American theme in honour of Britney. Cole hinted at which Britney song her act would be singing when she introduced her, saying, 'She's toxic, it's Alexandra Burke.'

The girl herself then reflected on her performance during the Take That show the previous weekend. 'Last week it was absolutely a dream come true, I had the best time. It just proved to me that this is what I want do for the rest of my life.' Commenting on

Walsh's comparison between her and Leona Lewis, the contestant said, 'For me it's unbelievable that he said that. If I could have a quarter of her success, I would die a happy woman.'

Cole smiled as she said, 'I've given Alexandra one of Britney's best, biggest and raunchiest songs. She's just going to go to town on it.'

Alexandra, too, was very excited by what was to come, bouncing up and down as she told the camera, 'Get this: Brian has given me fourteen dancers to dance with onstage.'

Brian himself indicated how much the stakes had been raised when he said, 'She's doing an iconic Britney song with the original choreography that I did for Britney. She's got to own it.'

Cole was in ebullient mood and threw down a warning to her fellow judges when she said, 'The other judges should be very worried tonight because Alexandra is going to once again steal the show.'

But Cowell threw the sentiment back at her when he said, 'It's too risky. I think there are other songs that would be safer for her.'

With this show effectively the quarter-finals, the tension was increasing and Alexandra concluded the VT by trying to express how she felt. 'This is my biggest challenge yet,' she said. 'I don't wanna leave a week before the semi-finals and, if I did, that would kill me.'

It was a fantastic performance. Alexandra was every bit as good a mover as Britney and sang the song 'Toxic' brilliantly. She drew the by now customary passionate applause from the audience and judges.

As usual, Irishman Walsh was the first to speak. 'Alexandra Burke, I said last week you're the best girl since Leona,' he said. 'If there's any justice, you have to be in the final of *The X Factor*. I loved everything about it, the singing, the dancing, the styling. You're living your dream, it's so obvious and you've got star quality.'

Danni Minogue praised the entire performance of all involved but was in no doubt as to who the star had been. 'Alex, that was one of Britney's most iconic tracks and I couldn't think of anyone better to do that song. The dancers were amazing but you never let them upstage you. Brilliant.'

As for Cowell, he had said that the song choice was unwise but he was big enough to admit that she pulled it off. 'Well, I've got to say, Alexandra, to choose that song and that routine the week before the semi-final was risky but it worked,' he said. 'This wasn't just a great performance within a talent competition, it was a great performance full-stop. If we were going to vote this on talent rather than popularity, there's no reason why you shouldn't be in the final. I'm very, very impressed.'

Cole, too, gave a nod to the danger that had been inherent in the song choice but had no doubt that Alexandra pulled it off. 'I know we took a risk, Alexandra, and I know you were very unsure about it at the beginning of the week,' said the Geordie. 'That was absolutely out of this planet. I absolutely loved it.'

Again, there had been a clean sweep of praise from the judges. Week after week, Alexandra was winning their approval. There was beginning to be a definite feeling that here was the winner. O'Leary, too, was full of praise. 'Wooh! Somebody just nailed that – I loved that,' he said.

Alexandra had received a lot of praise but she was quick to hand some out herself. With typical graciousness, she said, 'I want to say thanks to Brian because you just gave me some wicked choreography. We weren't worried about the vocals, just the dancing and having fun, and shaking what Britney's done.'

She had earlier been interviewed backstage, where she attempted to put into context how her growing fame was affecting her. 'Since I started this show, the attention has been quite enormous and quite overwhelming, to be honest,' she said. 'It's quite cool because it shows me I have so much support. Even just then in the corridor a girl asked me for my autograph for her nan and I thought that was really sweet! So it's been quite interesting how many people want to get to know us now because a year ago this wasn't happening. It's really good.'

Fellow contestant Ruth Lorenzo – with whom she was building a growing friendship – said, 'It takes her three hours to just like walk down the street, go somewhere and have lunch and come home even if it's five minutes away because people keep stopping us. Alex and I keep saying, "Oh, my God!"'

Alexandra added, 'I miss my mumma! I know when the final comes round I'm going to have a drink. Not had a drink for a while.'

Later in the show she returned to sing the Beyoncé hit 'Listen', which she had first sung at the judges'-houses phase. With its lyrics about dreams being realised and not pushed aside, it was again a truly fitting song for Alexandra to perform. This she did with gusto, producing one of the most memorable three-minute sessions of the entire series. No wonder she got a standing ovation from the entire audience and all four judges at the end. Her mentor Cole was so proud and moved that she shed tears. So did Alexandra.

Walsh said, 'Alexandra! That was incredible. It just doesn't get any better than that. You sing, you dance, you perform – you've got it all. You are the best girl singer in this competition. By a mile, by a mile.'

Minogue added, 'Alex, with that performance you deserve to be in the final. Please vote for Alex.'

Cowell, meanwhile, was about to deliver one of the most memorable judges' verdicts of the entire series. 'Alex, you know this is a British competition and you make me very proud to be British,' he said. 'It may sound like I'm favouring you tonight but you've really got to me. You're nineteen, twenty years old. I know what this means to you. I like people who try and I like people who are decent off-camera, which you've been throughout the competition. I think, taking every performance into account throughout the whole series, that was the best of the entire series.'

Emotions were running high and Cole seemed particularly choked up by the drama. 'I'm speechless,' she said. 'I'm so proud of you, Alexandra, and if I can't get you into the final it will be one of the biggest regrets of my career. I'm so proud of you and you grow in front of my eyes. You're just a little darling and I absolutely love you.'

Alexandra, too, was crying at this point and O'Leary summed up the mood by saying, 'It's like a big tear-fest tonight, are you all right?'

Through her emotion, Alexandra said, 'I just want to say to Cheryl, thank you for trusting me with such a big song, and for believing in me and carrying me this far. Thank you to those who voted and, Cheryl, you're a big inspiration to me, and my backbone, so thank you.'

In reflective mood, O'Leary said to her, 'Listen,

honey, I met you all those months ago at the Emirates Stadium and you said nobody understands what this means to you; what does this mean to you?'

With her emotion choking her up, Alexandra said, 'It means absolutely the world to me. I know everybody works hard and everybody has troubles but I'll tell you something, I've never, ever given up and this is the only thing I'll do for the rest of my life.'

Then it was time for the results. With just five contestants left and only four going through to the semi-finals, the atmosphere was extraordinarily tense as the results were handed to Dermot. Finally, he said the words Alexandra wanted to hear: 'The next contestant through to the semi-finals is... Alexandra Burke.'

Cue more emotions, outbursts and tears. It had been an emotional night. Although Britney Spears had not mingled with the contestants backstage, for all of them to see the reaction she got for her performance was a real shot in the arm. Could they be so iconic one day themselves? Alexandra later said of Britney's performance on the night, 'I think it was a really good performance for her first comeback. She got really slated and I feel sorry for her. She seems like a genuine, nice person.'

Only four acts could go through to the final. They were JLS, Alexandra, Eoghan Quigg and Diana Vickers. Which meant it was time for Spanish songstress Ruth Lorenzo to leave the competition. It was a sad moment for her and for Alexandra too. The two had become close friends and hated to be parted. However, Lorenzo wished Alexandra well and would be backing her in the following week's semi-finals. Which was where Alexandra reflected on the Britney week. 'Everyone in their lives has a moment where everything clicks into place and for me last week was my moment,' she said. '[The praise] means the world to me. It really makes me want this more and work harder, and makes me more determined to fight for what I want. My life has changed drastically since all this began. It has been the best time of my life and I would never give up anything for it. I was the girl who was chucked out three years ago and to think I'm sitting a week away from the final. I just can't fail now, I have to make it to the final.'

Again, each act would deliver two performances. Introducing the first, Cole said confidently, 'Alexandra can sing and dance – fact. Tonight, with this first song, she's going to absolutely smash it.'

Cowell, however, was not quite as convinced. 'Here's the problem: how can you top what she did last week? There's a lot of pressure on Alexandra for the first time because suddenly all eyes are on this girl.'

The young lady herself said, 'I'm in touching

distance of what I've dreamed of all my life and I just cannot let this go.'

It was showtime! The song she was singing was 'Don't Stop The Music' by Rihanna. Alexandra's performance of it was heavily choreographed with herself and a troupe of dancers following an eyecatching, complicated routine. Towards the end, the song segued into the 'Mama-se, mama-sa, mama-coo-sa' Michael Jackson chant from 'Wanna Be Startin' Somethin''. At the song's conclusion, a tickertape shower covered the stage. Alexandra looked triumphant. If there had been pressure on her going into the song, it wasn't showing.

Walsh was massively positive in his feedback, particularly considering that he mentored JLS, who were potentially her biggest rivals. 'Alexandra Burke, last week you were incredible. Tonight you're just as good. You sing, you dance – you've got everything. I think for the first time England is going to have a girl like Beyoncé or Whitney. You've got everything and you must make the final. You have to.'

Minogue by this time had no act left in the competition so was a neutral judge. She said, 'Fiiiieeeerce performance! That was so great to see! So strong, so sexy – loved everything about it.'

Cowell had a cheeky twinkle in his eye as he said, 'Alex, watching that film beforehand, it just reminded me how Louis nearly wrecked your life three years ago. You needed a break, he crushed your dreams.'

Walsh jumped in with, 'She wasn't ready, Simon. That's why I didn't pick her.'

Cowell countered, 'She was. What's happening is that we may be seeing the birth of a star here. I said it last week, I'm going to say it again. You want to find someone British, somebody you can be proud of and who can represent you around the world. I think you've got it all – that was a great performance.'

Cole echoed all this praise: 'Simon just took the words right out of my mouth. Do you know what? That was the best performance of an up-tempo song. You had fire in your belly and there's nothing else to say – I love you!'

O'Leary fairly bounced back to centre-stage and said, 'Pressure? What pressure?'

Alexandra laughed and nodded in agreement, saying, 'You know what? Because I kept saying this could be my last performance on the show, I'm going to enjoy myself. You never know! I have to say thank you to Louis for putting me out three years ago because I wouldn't be the person I am today if he hadn't.'

However, this was just the first of the two songs Alexandra would perform on the night. Cole introduced the second one, promising it was 'one of the most beautiful songs ever written'.

Alexandra added, 'This second song is so important for me to get so right because I cannot afford to make any mistakes.'

Cole said, 'This song is huge and even for Alexandra it's a massive challenge. I want Alexandra to go out there and show everybody she truly deserves that place in the final.'

Then it was time for the final word on the VT, which went as ever to the contestant. 'Getting to the end means the world to me,' said Alexandra with steel in her eyes. 'I will fight – anything that stands in my way has to go.'

The song was 'Unbreak My Heart' by Toni Braxton, which reached number 10 on the Billboard Hot 100 All-Time Top Songs and number 3 on the Top Billboard Hot 100 R&B/Hip-Hop Songs. Alexandra's fantastic performance of it earned her another standing ovation.

'Alexandra Burke, you are an incredible performer, an incredible singer, an incredible person,' raved Walsh. 'You are in a different league to most singers we've ever had in this competition. You deserve to be in the final. I know you as a person and I think you're absolutely incredible.'

Minogue agreed: 'Alex, you are a star. You have fought with two of the most incredible performances tonight and you have to be in the final. Please vote. Please vote Alex!'

This was Burkemania again. Surely she would make the final.

What did Cowell think? 'You know, Alex, I don't like to say this but, after the first round, because everyone was so strong, it occurred to me that you could leave this competition tonight. But that song might have changed everything. You know, that is one of the hardest songs. That's why nobody has sung this song before. You've got guts, you've got talent. If it is a talent competition you have to make it to the final and I hope people vote for you, Alex. It was outstanding.'

Cole then gave her final verdict of the evening. This was her last chance to not just canvass for votes, but also to pay tribute to her act. 'Alexandra, if there's any justice in this world, you'll get through to the final but we all know that this competition is so unpredictable. I want to take this opportunity to say thank you so much for making my first appearance on the show so enjoyable, exciting. I just find you the most incredible person to work with. I absolutely love you to pieces and I pray to God that we're here next week talking about the same thing. Thank you so much.'

All that love was more than reciprocated by Alexandra. 'Cheryl, you know you are my backbone,' she said emotionally. 'I have a message to everybody in the world watching: never give up on your dreams because if I had given up on mine three years ago I wouldn't be here today.'

O'Leary asked, 'Just one quick question: if you could say anything to you three years ago now, what would it be?'

Alexandra reflected briefly and replied, 'Just to have more fun because I was too serious back then. Now I have fun and enjoy what I do. I enjoy life now.'

The delivery of the results in the semi-final is always a particularly tense moment. O'Leary joined the remaining contestants on the stage, told them that over two million votes had been cast and announced that the first act through was JLS, who positively romped in celebration. Alexandra was the next act announced as through, and she sank to her knees in celebration. Next through was young Irishman Eoghan Quigg, which meant that his beloved Diana Vickers would be going home. She was given the chance to sing a farewell song and chose 'White Flag' by Dido. She sung it magnificently, its lyrics seeming to fit the moment rather well. As the song neared its conclusion, young Quigg – who had become enormously fond of Vickers during the show, sparking rumours of a romance between the pair – ran on to the stage, moved her away from the microphone and hugged her. The other contestants joined soon after and the sound of tears all round emanated from their microphones.

It was an enormously emotional end to the semi-final. However, their sadness at the departure of Vickers could not conceal the joy Alexandra and the other three finalists felt that they had made it through. It was going to be quite an evening in seven nights' time.

CHAPTER TEN

THE
FINAL

Alexandra stood on the brink of *X Factor* glory, with her place in the final assured. However, a storm was brewing that threatened to destroy her dreams. An ex-boyfriend of Alexandra's was trying to make trouble for her in the papers. It was very unpleasant stuff and, as a friend of Alexandra's claimed, the ex's behaviour had become quite disturbing of late. An unnamed friend said, 'It's almost two years since Alex split and she has more than moved on – but he never has. Now she's on the brink of the big time he's bombarding her with text messages saying he loves her and wants her back. Last Thursday he sent her a text that spelled out he *knew* she was at the TV studios in London, adding, "Nice brown jacket." Alex was really spooked by that because he was obviously watching her. She *was* at the studios and she *was* wearing a brown jacket. Alex is already a worrier. Now she can hardly sleep with the stress. It seems he has somehow found out her schedule and tracks her movements.'

As for the ex, he attempted to garner sympathy for himself by telling the *News Of The World* how upset he was after the couple split. 'I was destroyed when Alex broke up with me,' he said, sniffing. 'I'd text her 20 times a day. I was suicidal.' He denied suggestions that his messages were threatening, although he did admit, 'Some of them were angry like when anyone argues.' He continued, 'I'm still in love with Alex and I've told her that many a time. I'm still hoping to get back together with her. But apparently she's going out with one of these JLS boys. I heard it before I even read it in the paper. I've got my spies everywhere. I'm the main ex-boyfriend who knows everything. Everything about everything.'

However, Alexandra was not going to let this beat her. She simply steeled herself and doubled her determination to win *The X Factor*. Her mother Bell said, 'They broke up two years ago and she came back to live at home with me. They lived together for just under a year and were together about 18 months before that. He was possessive. He went everywhere with her. She hasn't spoken to him for almost two years. She won't see him or meet with him, or return his calls or texts.'

Alexandra had no choice but to try to ignore this controversy and focus on the final of *The X Factor*. There she would perform the winner's single. This year the producers had chosen the song 'Hallelujah', written by Leonard Cohen. Originally released in 1984, the song has taken on a whole life of its own, having been covered countless times and recorded on at least 180 occasions. Some of these versions have been good, others bad, others ugly, as Bryan Appleyard wrote in *The Times*: 'The story of one particular song that seems, through some mysterious alchemy, to have done everything a modern song can do. Leonard Cohen's "Hallelujah" has been papped, drivelled, exploited and massacred. It has also produced some very great performances, and it is, in truth, a very great song. In a fundamental sense, at least partly intended by Cohen, it is a song about the contemporary condition of song.

'Even if you think you haven't heard it, I can guarantee you have. It has been covered by, among many others, Allison Crowe, kd lang, Damien Rice, Bono, Sheryl Crow and Kathryn Williams. Bob Dylan has sung it live, a performance that has, apparently, been bootlegged. It has been used in films and on television. Rufus Wainwright sang it on the soundtrack of *Shrek*, Jeff Buckley's version was used on *The West Wing* and *The OC*, John Cale sang it on *Scrubs*, and so on. Cale's is the best version I have heard — pure, cold and scarcely inflected at all, it sends shivers down the spine.'

One strong fan of the song is *X Factor* judge Louis Walsh, who says, 'I have ten versions of it on my iPod – I particularly love kd lang's version. Everybody says Jeff Buckley's is the best version but I prefer Cohen's. Rufus's is OK too.'

It took Cohen nearly a year to write the song, which he described as the most challenging songwriting experience of his life. It was soon to become the subject of a major controversy too. Fans of Buckley's version united on the Internet to try to prevent *The X Factor* cover becoming a hit, while a Facebook group was started to try to rally sales for the Buckley cover, in the hope they could outsell *The X Factor* winner's version. The group's mandate read, 'Following the rather depressing news that this year's *X Factor* finalist will be covering Leonard Cohen's beautiful "Hallelujah", I think everyone should download the Jeff Buckley version, instead of buying the inevitably soulless version churned out by Simon Cowell's Crimbo flash in the pan... We can make this work, and make a huge statement against the barrage of cynical manufactured pop dirtying up our charts. I am willing to download this version the week the *X Factor* version comes out, and I know others will be too.'

The group, Jeff Buckley's 'Hallelujah' Christmas

Number One, urged its 360 members: '"Hallelujah" by Jeff Buckley is one of the most amazing covers of all time and now the *X Factor* winner is releasing their version as a Christmas single. Please boycott it. Do not buy this pop, over-produced and heartless version of perhaps one of the most poetic songs of the last century. Buy Jeff Buckley's version on iTunes for 79p.'

Meanwhile, Stop The X-Factor losers releasing Leonard Cohen's 'Hallelujah' as a single group, which has nearly 900 members, contends that, 'Even if we can't prevent this travesty we can at the very least make our revulsion known.'

Gordon Smart, writing in the *Sun*, said, 'The battle for the Christmas No2 single is well and truly upon us. *The X Factor* winner is nailed-on for No1 with their cover of "Hallelujah". But today I join the campaign to get another version of "Hallelujah" into second spot. The late American singer-songwriter Jeff Buckley's mesmerising 1994 cover of the Leonard Cohen song showcases the track at its brilliant best.'

The irony seemed lost on them that both Buckley's version and that of the eventual *X Factor* winner were on the same record label. Therefore, their campaign was only filling the coffers of those behind *The X Factor* version.

Alexandra ignored all this. 'I'm in the final, I literally cannot believe it,' she screeched on the first VT of her big night. 'It's absolutely incredible!' She was shown wearing a fantastic pink jacket and black trousers combo as she left the hotel and stepped into the stretch limo that would take her home to North London for the traditional pre-final visit. 'I remember thinking, Oh, my goodness, is that for me?' she said, smiling.

First up on the day had been a Heart FM radio interview and then it was on to her primary school. As she stepped out, she was mobbed by excited kids. 'I felt like I was swamped, it was the most incredible feeling.' She sang to the kids in assembly. 'I've always been inspired as a kid, you know? For me to inspire anyone to live their dreams and never give up, that puts a smile on my face.' Then she was shown returning home. 'To see them all and then to give them all the biggest hug was just the best feeling ever.'

Her sister told her, 'It just makes me so proud, you know? To hear people say your name.'

Alexandra was just as loving. 'Being back with my sister and sitting together on the bed that we used to share just felt so beautiful to me because my sister really cares. Not many people can say they have a sister that is their best friend. '

Next up on her pre-final jaunt was a performance in her native North London. 'In the evening it was ridiculous. I literally stepped out of the limo and felt like I was a movie star.'

She was pictured leaving the limo at the Koko

venue in Camden, North London. Screaming crowds had lined up to ask for photographs with her and to ask for her autograph. 'It was crazy,' she said. She was then shown walking on to the stage at Koko to a hysterical welcome. Burkemania had hit North London. She described that experience as the best moment of her life. 'I didn't give up on my dream three years ago, and walking on to that stage and the feeling I got was the reason why. I just had the most incredible day of my entire life. I just feel like I can touch my dream and I really, really want to win this.'

But to win it she would need to perform strongly at the final.

And she certainly started well. Her first song of the evening was 'Silent Night'. Wearing a stunning white dress, with white lights illuminating her from behind and white candles set up on stage, she looked suitably virginal to sing such a holy song. In classic Alexandra style, she slowly and soulfully built the song until the end when, joined by a backing choir, she was almost ripping the roof off *The X Factor* studio with her voice.

As ever, Walsh was the first to deliver his verdict. 'Alexandra Burke, you absolutely look like a superstar tonight,' he said. 'I knew you'd make the final, you've got an incredible personality and you're going to have a massive career in music, I absolutely know that.'

Then came the Minogue judgement: 'A platinum performance by anyone's standards. Get used to the red carpets and the limos because you are our *X Factor* songstress superstar.'

Cowell took the praise to a new level. 'Alexandra, I've got to say that was outstandingly good.' He smiled. 'I mean, come on! I know how much this means to you. I mean, you almost had your life wrecked by Louis three years ago. You've come back, no whining, no complaining, on the biggest night of your life. That was, by any standard, outstanding!'

It was time for her mentor Cole to wrap up the first round of comments. 'Alexandra, we said from the start, no expectations, just high hopes – and I have got the highest hopes for you tonight. I absolutely love you to pieces and I want the end result to be the right result, which is to see you up there. I absolutely love you to pieces. I love you, love you, love you.'

Presenter O'Leary then asked Alexandra how she felt.

'Words cannot describe how I feel right now,' she began. 'I'm so overwhelmed by the support I've seen and I'm just so grateful and honoured to be on this stage, and I have to thank you guys so much.'

At the North London venue where supporters of Alexandra had gathered, former Hear'say singer Kym Marsh was doing an outside broadcast for the show. 'I'm here with hundreds of Alexandra fans and Alexandra fever has hit.'

Schoolfriends and former teachers of Alexandra gave their praise against a backdrop of cheering North Londoners.

However, it was too early for anyone to celebrate, as this was just the first of Alexandra's songs on the night. Next up it was time for her duet with Beyoncé, which would caused quite a stir on the night. Alexandra began the song alone. Wearing a sleek silver dress that glittered and revealed plenty of leg, she sang the first verse beautifully. This was her third performance of the song in the series and, as she completed the first chorus, it was time for her to say the words she never thought would be possible. 'Ladies and gentlemen,' she said, with her voice trembling, 'please welcome my hero, Beyoncé.'

The shapely superstar sauntered on with a positively regal presence. She gave Alexandra a protective look, took her hand and launched into the second verse. They then sang successive lines, still holding hands. As Beyoncé handed over to Alexandra, she memorably beckoned her: 'Sing it, GIRL!' Golden glitter cascaded on to the stage as the pair brought the song to a simply astonishing climax.

As the audience erupted, Alexandra was overcome by emotion. She collapsed on to her hero's shoulder, sobbed and shook. Even the judges' panel was overcome by the moment, with Cole and Cowell embracing.

'What... a moment,' exclaimed O'Leary. 'Ladies and gentlemen, Alexandra and Beyoncé!' He then thanked Beyoncé for being a part of the show and said, 'First things first, what do you think of our girl?'

Beyoncé coolly said, 'She's a superstar. Such a beautiful voice, such a beautiful young lady. I'm very happy to sing with you.'

But at this praise, it all got too much for Alexandra. 'Thank you so much,' she said as she gave in to the tears and sobs that she had been trying to hold back. 'Oh, God, you've made my dreams come true,' she said through the sobs. 'Thank you for making Cheryl's too because we was fighting for this and I love you so much.'

Beyoncé then mentioned she was touring the UK in 2009 and that she hoped to see Alexandra then.

'Just stay,' joked O'Leary. 'Stay round at Alexandra's. She'll have you, don't worry about it.'

It had been a spectacular duet and, if there was a performance that won it for Alexandra, then this was it. In comparison, JLS's duet with Westlife and Quigg's with Boyzone were markedly inferior. The tide had turned in favour of Alexandra and she was surely headed for victory. As for the girl herself, she was just overjoyed to have met another of her heroines. Consequently, at this point she already felt like she had died and gone to heaven, regardless of whether she won. 'I only met her at five-thirty on Saturday afternoon. I met her in the dressing room and I cried on her shoulders for five minutes,' she later said.

While it's fair to say she did not 'play it cool' when they met, doesn't that just add to her charm?

'Then I started to go on about how much I loved her and how much she had changed my life, it was so embarrassing! Then her mum Tina started crying and I gave her a hug. I asked if I could be on her tour and she said yes, so we'll see what happens.'

Back onstage at *The X Factor*, in front of the nation, she sang 'You Are So Beautiful' as her choice of reprise from earlier episodes.

Walsh praised her 'very emotional performance' and told her, 'You were fantastic.'

After describing the atmosphere as 'absolutely electric', Minogue said she loved the way that Alexandra picked up on the emotion of the song. 'You took it to a different level,' she continued.

Cowell said, 'Alexandra – for whatever reason, you haven't had the right breaks in your life. I don't understand that. But tonight I am going to predict that a star has been born. Tonight I just felt something special from you. Maybe it's your determination, your passion or just because you're very talented. Your family are going to be very proud of you tonight.'

Cole then thanked the public for voting for Alexandra and also thanked the programme makers for making her feel so welcome herself.

'Alexandra,' she continued, 'you have made this the most special night of my life and I am so incredibly proud of you. I can't even put it into words. The icing on the cake would be to see you crowned *X Factor* winner.'

Then it was time to return to the North London post where Marsh was joined by hundreds of Alexandra fans. Bedlam was continuing there and there was a real feeling in the air that victory was on its way for Alexandra. Back in the main studio, as O'Leary gave out the numbers for people to call to vote for Alexandra, she told him she loved him.

But would the public love her enough for her to win? She had one last chance to secure the public vote, when she sang the winner's single 'Hallelujah'. With her gold dress, a backing choir and a white star light behind her, she looked positively heavenly and spiritual. At the song's conclusion, she got a standing ovation from everyone present. That was it, she had done all she could do and would now have to see what the public thought in the final vote.

But before then the judges gave their final feedback to this emerging star. Walsh said, 'Alexandra, I love that song, I love your interpretation. You've got everything it takes to be a star and from tonight you're going to be a big recording artist, I know that.'

Minogue told her, 'Alex, you are the voice of the

2008 singing competition. That was strong and it was gentle, and it was sincere – your best performance.'

Cowell again pounced on the chance to ham it up and take the evening to a whole new level. Looking genuinely stunned, he said, 'I'm sorry – that was unbelievable!' As the audience roared its approval, he added, 'That was just... I mean, seriously – incredible! You've got to win. Incredible.'

Cole said, 'I can't find any words to say to you other than, over the past six months we've become more than a mentor and an act. You're my friend and I just hope this all ends the way it should, and you are the winner in my eyes.'

Alexandra then took one last opportunity to canvass for some votes. 'You don't understand,' she said, 'to everyone who has kept me in the final two, thank you so much. I'm so honoured to be on this stage and it's been the best experience of my life. Thank you, thank you so much.'

So it came to the results: who had won the show? Quigg had already been voted out earlier in the show, so it was between Alexandra and JLS for the title of X Factor winner.

O'Leary announced, 'I can tell you tonight we've had eight million votes, thank you so much. And the people of Britain have decided that the winner of The X Factor 2008 is...'

Then came the traditional, excruciating pause as

the camera panned between the two final acts: JLS and Alexandra.

As she waited to hear who had won, Alexandra will have been grateful and proud of how far she had come. She was friendly with JLS and was pleased to have made the final two. However, she is an ambitious and focused person so she will have been determined to win. As O'Leary drew the pause out further and further, the tension in her grew and grew. Anyone would feel it in her shoes but, for Alexandra, an emotional young woman, the pressure will have been immense. She clenched her face and looked at the floor.

Even as they waited, audience members shouted out her name. Surely she was going to win? However, she couldn't know at all until O'Leary completed his sentence. The show had seen more than its fair share of shocks in this series. Nothing could be taken for granted.

On and on the pause went until O'Leary finally completed the sentence, shouting, 'Alexandra!'

The shocked expression of the winner will for ever be a part of classic *X Factor* history. She looked stunned and then collapsed to her knees as the tickertape came down and the audience roars almost ripped the roof off the studio. Cole then triumphantly lifted her act up and the two of them danced a jig of celebration. The taunts from the bullies, the testing childhood and the rejection from this very show three years earlier all lifted from Alexandra's shoulders as she danced in celebration. She was literally shrugging it all off and standing tall as the champion of *The X Factor*. She had done it – hallelujah!

'Alexandra, congratulations,' said O'Leary. 'Cheryl, congratulations as well.'

Meanwhile, Alexandra walked to JLS and gave them consoling hugs. O'Leary asked Alexandra how she felt and her initial attempts to answer were so choked up with emotion as to be incomprehensible. 'Alex, can you talk for me or not, hun?' asked O'Leary. 'Come on, baby, if you can sing you can talk,' he added encouragingly.

'Thank you,' she managed, then added, 'I feel like I'm gonna faint. Thank you, everyone. Thank you to Simon, Danni, Louis Cheryl, Nigel, Brian...' She then trailed off as the shock, emotion and joy once more rose to the surface.

'Baby, I'm just going to give you a little bit of time to compose yourself,' said O'Leary before commiserating with JLS.

Returning to Alexandra, he said, 'This really is the stuff that dreams are made of. Come here, you. Not only have you just won a recording contract, but I can tell you that Alexandra will be performing at the O2 arena on New Year's Eve with Elton John. Your debut single is available for download tonight and will be available in the shops from Wednesday.' He showed Alexandra a copy of the CD.

'Oh, my God,' said Alexandra with her nerves showing no sign of abating. 'To everyone who voted for me, this is for you and I swear to God, this is for you.'

It was then time for her to sing her debut single, as the winner. At times during her performance, the nerves interrupted her vocals, but always in a way that – in the moment – added to, rather than detracted from, the quality of her performance. Towards the end of the song, her fellow finalists joined her on the stage and their sheer joy for her in victory was palpable. The judges, too, looked on with delight, Cowell and Cole cuddling with a mixture of joy, relief and pride. At the song's ending, she was surrounded by her fellow finalists.

Cowell took the opportunity to have a final say about the series in general as well as the result. 'Look, I am rarely speechless but I am now. Alex, God bless you, you deserved it. Cheryl, I'm very proud of you, kid. I know this isn't everyone's cup of tea, this show but, to everyone who has watched it, voted for it and written about it, thank you so much.'

Then Alexandra was allowed one final word. 'Thank you for making my dreams come true everyone and, my God, I am the happiest girl alive.

Cheryl, I have everything to thank you for. Everything, and thanks to Beyoncé.'

The show was over but there was still the ITV2 sister show *The Xtra Factor* to be broadcast. There, Alexandra gave her first interview as winner. Presenter Holly Willoughby introduced Alexandra, and did the quizzing of the winner and her mentor. Asked what the following year held in store for Alexandra, Cole said, 'She's just going to go global. There's no question about it. We went in to see Beyoncé, who is the most gracious humble superstar you could want to meet. She has everything marked on the cards for Alexandra to be a huge superstar.'

Alexandra joked that she now wanted another duet with Beyoncé. She was shown the footage of the moment when her victory was announced. On seeing it back, she commented that her shock was genuine and that all night she had believed it was between Eoghan and JLS for victory. She then beckoned her fellow contestants, 'Please, everyone, we have to have a party.' She then told the pregnant Willoughby that she must call her baby Alexandra if she had a girl, or Alex if she had a boy. A typical Alexandra quip.

Then it was off to the backstage press conference where Alexandra sat hand in hand with her mentor and now friend Cheryl Cole, as she faced the nation's journalists. The assembled reporters who crowded into the press lounge were excited by Alexandra's arrival. The winner told them, 'I'm in such shock. I thought it was between JLS and Eoghan. I'm in disbelief. Honestly, I keep saying to my family, "This isn't real." I cannot believe what's just happened to my life.'

Cole admitted that she went to Simon Cowell's dressing room to do a dance of victory.

Naturally, Alexandra's duet with Beyoncé was one of the key talking points of the press conference. The winner tried to put it all in context. 'We start at this point – during the week, nothing was confirmed,' she said. 'Then it was Friday night and it was "By the way, you're singing with Beyoncé." I literally cried on her shoulder in the dressing room, telling her how she's changed my life, how much I love her. Words cannot describe how I felt. I nearly cried when I introduced her onstage. She is the most humbling person.'

A reporter asked Cole whether she was jealous that she had not had the chance to duet with such a legend. 'Jealous? Not at all.' laughed Cole. 'Me on stage with Beyoncé? I would have hit the deck! I wouldn't have been able to sing. I was more than happy that it was Alexandra. For her to stand there and be able to get a note out was amazing.'

Her sick mother's presence at the final had been another point of interest in the press conference and Alexandra was asked what it meant to her. 'It means the world to me that my mum could make it,' she replied. 'She said, "Even if they have to drag me from my bed, I will make the show." She's probably tired now but it means the world to me that she was here. In week one, I cried because I looked into the audience and she wasn't there. My mum, I don't think she realises how much she means to me.'

Another media interest that had built up around Alexandra was the inevitable comparison between her and former *X Factor* winner Leona Lewis. 'If I could have an inch of her career, I would be a happy person,' said Alexandra. 'My gosh, she came from Hackney and she's done what she's done. That is just unreal and, you know what, she's a true inspiration to me. I want to follow in her footsteps. I feel honoured to have stood on the same stage as Leona Lewis.'

Ever the witty performer, Alexandra then declared, 'I want a duet with Girls Aloud!'

Cole quipped in return, 'No! You'll upstage us!' The pair clearly had a deep rapport, as Cole explained. 'We clicked from the off and then we grew as she had tantrums and wobbles. Before "Candyman", she had the biggest wobble ever. It's all those things people don't see, the contact we have with each other.'

Alexandra agreed, saying, 'Cheryl bought me the best present ever to protect me. No, I'm saying it. It's an angel-wing diamond and it's so beautiful. I'm going to wear it every day and it's going to protect me. Thanks to Cheryl, I love you.' Finally, Alexandra almost burst with joy when discussing her forthcoming appearance on the *Top Of The Pops Xmas Special*. 'I've got to tell the world, right? Earlier this year I told my mum, "I can't believe *Top Of The Pops* has stopped the show!" I wanted to be on it and I cried when they stopped that show. Then they told me that *The X Factor* winner would perform on a special one-off *Top Of The Pops*. That's what kicked me up the bum and told me, "You'd better win, girl!"'

As for her mother, she was having a ball backstage. 'Simon Cowell was ecstatic and he gave me a glass of champagne. I took one sip but then his ex-girlfriend, Terri Seymour, took my glass, saying, "You're not supposed to drink." I hugged Cheryl and there was a real party atmosphere. I felt relief. I'm so happy I don't have to see my daughter struggle any more. She immediately said that she wanted to buy me my own dialysis machine, but I refused. I worked in the music business long enough to know that it will be a year before Alexandra will see any money and you can never guarantee that fame or fortune will last. But her life has changed. I don't think she'll ever live at home again but she will always be my little girl.'

Her little girl was about to enter the promotional whirlwind that befalls *The X Factor* winner. One of the first journalists to spend time with Alexandra in the aftermath of the show was the *Guardian*'s Simon Hattenstone. Perhaps the nation's leading newspaper interviewer, Hattenstone is a journalistic legend, and that he had been put on to Alexandra's case by the *Guardian* spoke volumes about her status as *X Factor* winner. He wrote, 'Burke is 20, beautiful, and looks permanently startled. On Saturday, she looked startled when her hero Beyoncé Knowles joined her to sing a duet, and even more startled when she won after transforming Leonard Cohen's "Hallelujah" into a tremendous power ballad. When she sang it a second time, the tears fell so fast and heavy, her face began to dissolve in front of our eyes. By yesterday morning, the tears were staunched, but she still looked startled. She had slept for only an hour, her voice was reduced to a croak, and she was too bewildered to be tired. She changed into any number of outfits, shook up bottle after bottle of champagne like a formula-one driver, and squirted the fountains into the air triumphantly.'

He joined her on the morning after the final at 9am. There had been precious little rest for Alexandra. After the photoshoot, he and Alexandra stepped into a top-of-the-range BMW and an amusing incident ensued. 'The driver turned on the radio,' remembers Hattenstone. 'A song started out, gently. Burke was in a trance. She recognised the song, but she didn't believe it was on the radio. She thought it was a joke.

"What's that CD?" The driver assured her it was the radio. "No! Yes! Prove to me it's the radio." Finally, she was convinced. "Shit! Shit! Shit! Shit!" Every shit was more ecstatic than the previous. "Oh, my God! Oh, my God! Oh, my God. Stop swearing. Oh, my God! Mummmmm!" And she literally cried for her mother as they played her song. "Oh no, this moment should have been with my mum. This feeling is unreal. I'm just trying to get over last night and then this happens. It's the first time on the radio.'"

As he began his interview with Alexandra, he noted her reaction when her single came to its conclusion. 'On the radio, the song finished and Burke listened closely to the DJ. "That was London's Alexandra Burke and 'Hallelujah'. Were you a JLS fan or was Alexandra the right winner? I'd love to hear from you this morning. It's Capital at Christmas.'"

The *Top Of The Pops* visit was huge for Alexandra, as she explained, 'When they told me I was going to do *Christmas Top Of The Pops* I couldn't believe it. It's amazing. A dream come true. Another dream come true for me. I can tick off that list.' She was so full of enthusiasm, the coldest heart in the world could not fail to be moved by her. 'When I was eight or nine, I watched my mum appear on *Top Of The Pops*. And I decided, one day I want to do the same. I was devastated when they cancelled the series. Absolutely gutted. Appearing on there was always one of the ways to tell whether you have actually made it, I think.'

She also filmed the video for her single. On her official blog, she explained just how much this meant to her. 'We shot the video for "Hallelujah" the other week and it was the most brilliant experience. Shooting the video for "Hero" was one thing but this was a whole other experience. There were two thousand candles spread across the floor with me singing in the middle. When I walked in, I nearly started crying again – I was an emotional wreck. I'd never heard "Hallelujah" before and, at first, I was worried it wouldn't suit my voice but I worked at it and was totally thrilled at the result, and was like, "OMG: that's me on a record."' The resultant video was indeed amazing and rarely in pop history have candles been employed to more stunning effect.

A big story that erupted around her at this time was that Cheryl Cole had advised – or ordered, depending on which report you believed – Alexandra to steer clear from romances with men while she built her fame, especially as there were reports in the national press that focused on details of her past romances – details that were hotly disputed. As a result, Alexandra was only too happy to follow Cole's advice to avoid men for the moment. 'That's why I've given up on them completely,' she admits. What if a special guy turned up? 'Well, Cheryl would be the one to decide whether he was good enough for me,' she says.

'He'd have to pass the Cheryl test! I like a guy with a good personality. You've got to vibe with someone, that's the way to go.'

Asked about the television presenter James Corden, who had become an outspoken admirer and had bought her a £4,000 Cartier watch, she replied, 'Oh, my God, the papers can make such a big thing out of nothing! I guess he bought the watch because he thought it was special. We exchanged numbers when he came to *The X Factor* and we've been texting each other. I feel extremely grateful that he's doing what he's doing – saying nice things about me and sending me a gift – but we're just friends. He's a lovely guy but that's as far as it goes.' A quote attributed to Alexandra's mother suggested that Corden was 'besotted' but Alexandra quickly denied this quote, saying, 'No, it wasn't my mum who said that. I don't know where it's come from, but not from my mumma.

'I'd love to go on a date with James but it would only be for a friendly drink,' said Alexandra diplomatically. 'I was flattered that he gave me such an expensive gift but there's no romance.'

Many of those statements were reported by leading celebrity magazine *Now* and, in the same publication, Alexandra revealed some tough times she had been through with her mother in 2005, the year she first auditioned for *The X Factor*. 'Mum tried to live her dream through me. She wanted to run my career. But she's had her shot at fame. It's my time to show what I can do. I told her to let me do it my own way. There are lots of one-hit wonders out there and I don't want to be one of them. We went through a rough patch – we weren't talking. I had to get out of the house,' says Alex. Now, however, familial relations were far stronger, as mother watched daughter become a star on the promotional trail.

Next up for Alexandra on her PR jaunt was an appearance on landmark ITV show *LK Today* where she was interviewed by host Lorraine Kelly. At this point, she was being followed by the *Mirror* newspaper, which gave an insight into life behind the scenes. 'I'm running on adrenaline,' Alexandra told them. 'I've had hardly any sleep since winning on Saturday but I'm loving every second. This is my dream and I'm on an absolute high.

'I'm up and ready to go to *GMTV* at four-thirty in the morning – I've only ever been up this early to catch a flight. I've done *GMTV* twice but it feels surreal sitting on the sofa chatting to Fiona Phillips and then going to be interviewed by Lorraine Kelly. It's all very exciting but I'm not sure I could be up so early every day.

'As I leave the studios at nine-thirty in the morning, right after talking to Lorraine Kelly, I can't believe how many photographers are outside waiting for me.

It's mad! I pose for pictures and sign some autographs for *X Factor* fans. I still find it weird that people want my autograph. It feels really special because I've waited for this for so long. I'm in a car heading off to a hotel to do a series of TV interviews. Some of the paparazzi are following, which is a bit scary – I'm not used to all the attention. Still, I know that's part of my job now. Cheryl Cole, my mentor, has told me that even when I'm having an off-day I should always be polite. That's fine by me – it's not in my nature to be nasty or horrible. And I know the photographers are only doing their job.'

On arrival at the *GMTV* studios she spoke to Fiona Phillips and Ben Shephard – the latter a one-time presenter of *The Xtra Factor*. Phillips introduced Alexandra, saying she thought that she herself was possibly more excited than her guest by the prospect of the interview. 'Everything right now seems like a big blur to me,' admitted Alexandra. 'It's all a blur.' She admitted that she might have been a 'bit overwhelming' for Beyoncé during the live final, telling her how much she loved her. She revealed that she 'popped the question' to Beyoncé about a further duet and added that she wanted to do a duet with Lewis one day, and one with Girls Aloud too. Speaking of her mother, she said, 'I love my mummy so much, she's a strong woman.' Alexandra spoke of wanting to buy her mother a bungalow, as she was in need of a home without stairs. She later developed this thought, saying, 'I don't want people thinking I went on *The X Factor* just because my mum's really, really ill and I have to get her a kidney. But I do want to make a career so I can get her better treatment – and I do want a better life for me and my family, that's my main concern.'

Back at the *GMTV* studios, the 'Hallelujah' video was premiered and then Alexandra performed the song live in the studio. 'Always hold on to your dreams,' said Alexandra at the end of the interview. Then it was time for the Lorraine Kelly chat. The Scottish presenter is a broadcasting legend so for Alexandra this was the sort of interview she will have dreamed of. As she was ushered into the North London studios, she might have reflected that, although only a couple of miles from home, she was a million miles from the days of sharing a bed with her sister. She had made it – and in some style!

Speaking of style, Kelly kicked off the interview by mentioning how fantastic Alexandra looked. 'You really do,' said Kelly. She then reminded the winner just how emotional she got when her victory was announced: 'You cried and cried and cried!'

Alexandra laughed and said, 'Oh, my goodness, I have some more tears to give, believe you me,' and explained the emotion came from the fact that 'I made it this far – I didn't think I would.'

The moment of victory had been intense, not least because O'Leary naturally drew out the announcement slowly in order to create maximum tension. 'I was shouting at the telly, "Will you please put them out of their misery,"' said Kelly.

Alexandra agreed with the sentiment: 'It was the longest wait ever. Oh, my goodness. I'll never forget that moment.' This was just days after that victory but, as Alexandra told Kelly, she had already encountered a whole new set of work contacts. 'It's just been the most amazing fun,' she said. 'I've met the most fantastic people. All of *The X Factor* staff and everyone now at Sony and Syco. I've been surrounded by the most positive people and I could really not ask for more. I've made some amazing friends and I'm just so thankful for this experience and everything I'm going through.'

Kelly then turned the conversation to the immediate aftermath of Saturday's victory. What had happened? asked Kelly. A huge party?

'No partying – not for me,' said Alexandra. 'My family wouldn't leave the hotel I was staying in. My dad fell asleep. Everyone was talking, they got through three bottles of champagne and I sat with a cup of PG Tips.'

A cup of tea – how typically down to earth of Alexandra! This was noted with respect by Kelly, and another aspect of her interviewee's conduct that got the nod of approval from Kelly was the fact that she did not use her mother's illness as ammunition for votes during the show, only really touching on it after she had won.

'I just feel that music is my music and my personal life is my personal life,' said Alexandra by way of explanation. 'I'm so proud of my mum. She had her dialysis on Saturday and still made it down. She is on the waiting list for a transplant. But she's doing well. She's a strong woman.'

Alexandra also praised Cole. 'I don't even call her my mentor, she's my friend,' she said. 'A really close friend. We've connected deeply. She's now a really close friend of mine. I miss her already.'

A viewer called in to ask how the famously emotional Alexandra managed to avoid her make-up running. Was it waterproof mascara? suggested Kelly.

Alexandra laughed. 'Oh, my goodness, yes! Adam, the make-up artist on the show, knows that I can cry for England. So it's waterproof mascara all the way.'

Steering the interview back to the live final, Kelly said that, for her as a viewer, the Beyoncé duet was a key moment of drama.

'For me that was the biggest thing that's ever happened in my life,' said Alexandra. 'When I introduced her on the stage I had to hold myself together. I kept saying to myself, "If you start crying now, you'll lose that minute in the song." Even in rehearsal I had to hold myself back. I had to hold myself back, it was so magical.' She graciously paid tribute to the two runners up too. 'Eoghan and JLS were great on the night. I thought it was going to be between Eoghan and JLS.'

So what, wondered Kelly aloud, was Alexandra most looking forward to?

'Just everything,' replied the singer. 'Making the album and promoting the single, and just enjoying what there is to come. The moment I stop smiling is the day I'm going to give up. I want longevity. I told Simon on the show, "Are you ready because I'm going to work my socks off." I don't wanna break. No distractions – cups of tea and that's it.'

Kelly was clearly hugely respectful of Alexandra and concluded the interview saying, 'You're a worthy, worthy winner.'

A worthy winner indeed. After that interview, Alexandra's next stop was Radio One, where she was interviewed by Fearne Cotton. As she left the studio she found a mob of fans waiting outside to meet her. 'They were all waiting outside Radio One for me and that doesn't really fit well in my head,' she said.

Then she visited Great Ormond Street Children's Hospital. 'I'm shown round and introduced to patients on the wards by 16-year-old Bex Aspinall who has cerebral palsy – she's an absolute star,' she wrote in the *Mirror*. 'Meeting all these amazing children puts everything into perspective. I want to be strong for them. I will pray for them all. After leaving the hospital I'm in a hotel room having my hair and make-up done for the back-to-back TV interviews. If I look a bit shocked it's just that I was worried that exhaustion would kick in halfway through the interviews and I'd start flagging. As it turns out I have a great time, chatting away, and feel surprisingly lively. I've also got a camera crew from ITV2 following me round for *The Winner's Story*, which is on telly this Sunday.'

In the same week, HMV said that the 20-year-old's debut single was its fastest-ever-selling download. Spokesman Gennaro Castaldo said, 'It is not impossible that it will break the million mark. 'Over that would see it beat "Do They Know It's Christmas?" and claim the fastest-selling-single record title.'

In the first 24 hours it was on sale, it shifted 105,000 copies and went on to be the Christmas number one and the top-selling single of the year. No wonder there were high hopes for Alexandra behind the scenes. A source close to Simon Cowell said, 'He thinks Alexandra will be a big international star, if they get the music right. In many ways she is more versatile than Leona – she can really dance and there is a greater variety of things that she can do.'

Cowell's spokesman, Max Clifford, said, 'Simon is

a master at breaking acts in the UK and the American market. Alexandra is only twenty and she has come on leaps and bounds just over the course of the series. So imagine what she could do when she gets to work with the industry's best producers and writers. Asked if he was worried that Alexandra and Leona were too similar, Cowell himself said, "It is like asking, Would you want to sign up Whitney Houston when you already have Mariah Carey?" Of course you would. There is room for more than one female singer.'

'Hallelujah' stayed at number one for three weeks and made *The X Factor* winner the first British female solo artist to sell a million copies of a single in the UK. The track also became the biggest-selling single for a UK female solo artist in chart history, chart officials confirmed. Alexandra was blown away by all this success. 'Firstly, I have just been told that my single is number one,' she wrote on her blog. 'Wow! I need to actually take this all in at the moment. It still feels like I'm living in a dream. They told me that my song is the fastest-selling single by a female artist in UK history and it outsold the rest of the top 20 combined!!! I just can't believe this, six months ago I was going about my life trying to get a break doing little gigs here and there and this dream was a million miles away. Now the radio chart show have just called and said that I'm Christmas number one! Thank you, guys, sooooooooooooo much. I cannot explain how I am feeling and it is all down to your support. Thank you, thank you, thank you!!'

Martin Talbot, MD of the Official Charts Company, which compiles the figures, said, 'It is a particularly amazing week for Alexandra Burke, who has broken a string of records to announce her arrival in spectacular style.' Noting that the same song, 'Hallelujah', in its Buckley and Cohen manifestations charted in the same week at 2 and 36 respectively, he said these placings were 'remarkable for a 25-year-old song which has never previously reached the Top 40'.

Remarkable, indeed, as was Alexandra's growing stature. Her fame was being noted around the world, and rapper 50 Cent was soon sounding her out about a collaboration. A source said, 'Fiddy has been saying how talented she is. He wants her to star in his new music video.

'She's had loads of offers but 50 Cent is a huge name. This could instantly crack the US market for her. Leona Lewis has done it but not nearly as fast.'

Alexandra was also claiming that the legendary Beyoncé was up for a second duet with her. The future seemed full of possible collaborations; no wonder Alexandra was so excited.

First, though, Alexandra had a royal engagement to keep.

CHAPTER ELEVEN

INTO TOMORROW

Having already raised money for wounded soldiers with her part in the 'Hero' single, Alexandra was about to contribute once again. The *Sun* newspaper 'Millies' ceremony was hosted at Hampton Court Palace to award military men and women for their courage. The Prince of Wales, his wife Camilla, and a host of celebrities gathered to salute the winners and hand out the gongs. It was an emotional night, at turns inspiring and heartbreaking – and Alexandra was there to perform. But first, the Prince – who had come up with the idea of the Millies – addressing the 400-strong audience, said, 'This evening has given us the opportunity to meet the best of the best, the bravest of the brave. But please let us not forget that, as I speak, many members of our

Armed Forces are far away from their families, working in austere, challenging and often dangerous environments. It is right that we have them at the forefront of our minds this evening, and I offer my personal thanks and gratitude to them all.'

He later added, 'I suggested we might do this awards ceremony. Tonight we have heard some inspirational stories. Stories that I think prove our Armed Forces really are quite exceptional.'

Prime Minister Gordon Brown invited all the nominees to Downing Street to toast their courage, and told them, 'I am proud of you,' after presenting the Best Unit award to The Chinook Force in Afghanistan.

Summing up the spirit of the event, veteran entertainer Bruce Forsyth said, 'Isn't it fantastic that we can gather here tonight to recognise people who have actually done something with their lives?'

England and Chelsea football star Frank Lampard said, 'The word "hero" is used quite loosely these days but these are the real heroes.'

And actor Ross Kemp said, 'The night couldn't have gone better. I'm very proud to have been involved in this.'

After the awards, a minute's silence was held in honour of the dead.

Then it was time for Alexandra. A behind-the-scenes *Xtra Factor* documentary showed her as cool as a cucumber before taking to the stage. 'I'm about to perform in front of Prince Charles – so let's go!' she said. Wearing a tight-fitting black dress, she looked incredible and gave a fittingly emotional performance of the song 'Hero'. Like a true professional, she summed up the range of emotions that the night had evoked in the crowd and she sang beautifully of the heroes that lie in each of us. Previously she had shared the vocals on this song with the other *X Factor* finalists. However, here she was on her own and she took the song to a new level.

Afterwards, she was humble. 'On Tuesday, I was really honoured to be asked to perform at the Millies,' she wrote on her official blog. 'This is an awards show which supports our British troops. I sang *The X Factor* charity single "Hero", which means so much to me and it was great meeting with, in my opinion, our country's bravest people. Prince Charles was also there, which was pretty scary performing in front of him but it was great fun and such a brilliant event.'

It had not been her only generous act of the week, as she explained. 'I got to visit Great Ormond Street Hospital, which was incredible because I really love and admire children's charities, so it was great going down there and getting to meet all the nurses and children. It was really emotional but inspiring and the kids all seem so happy.'

And Alexandra confirmed the rumours of a new

friend in the svelte shape of Kate Moss. 'I saw Kate in the audience a couple of weeks ago and waved to her. I met her properly last week and we hit it off. I am going to her party on Friday. She promised me I could have anything I wanted from her wardrobe. She said I could stay the night then we would go for a pub lunch on Saturday. I can't wait.' She laughed off claims that Moss might corrupt her. 'I like a drink. Why not? Kate is a party girl but it is all good in the hood, if you ask me. She won't be leading me astray. She is a good person and we talked for ages. I met her daughter too. Kate and I talked about the show, her clothing line and things like that. I want to have my own range one day so it was interesting to hear what she had to say. I always bought her stuff anyway. The day it came out at Topshop I was at the front of the queue. She was giving me some fashion tips on what to wear. She said, "Always put your heels on and don't say 'yes' to every single item of free clothing."'

As Alexandra told *Grazia* magazine, the pair had quite a giggle together. 'I met her and her daughter, and her daughter's friend,' she remembered. 'They've got this little dance, this little handshake. Absolutely hilarious. Kate really wanted me to win from the beginning.' However, it seemed that Alexandra was not invited to the party after all. So Alexandra opted to head out with her mentor and friend Cheryl Cole instead. Not that she missed much. A source told the *Sun*, 'There were more last-minute cancellations than a Pete Doherty tour. Davina was ill but other excuses were lame. Kate spent the night apologising... for the turnout.'

Another famous name who was courting the attention of Alexandra at this time was Harrods owner Mohammed Al Fayed. As she revealed to *Grazia*, 'I said to Mohammed, "I want to launch my own clothing range – can I launch it in Harrods?" He said, "Maybe."'

The Egyptian-born retail tycoon invited her to the store and told her, 'I'm going to get my doctors to fly over to see your mother.' He was offering to cover all the costs of treatment for Alexandra's ill mother and also took her round the store, saying she could have anything she wanted for free.

An exciting experience for Alexandra – and for Al Fayed, who wrote on his official blog, 'I was delighted to welcome *X Factor* winner, Alexandra Burke, to Harrods this week when she came to do some out-of-hours shopping. She has a wonderful zest for life, and the combination of her enthusiasm and exceptional vocal talent will ensure that she has phenomenal success. Alexandra is already breaking records in the singles download charts, and was over the moon to see her single on the shelves in Harrods' HMV concession. She had never seen her single on display before! I take my hat off to this girl. Aged just 20, she has already handled the blows life has thrown at her with incredible maturity, bouncing back from difficulties presented to her with greater confidence, spirit and determination. I wish her, her mother and the rest of her family well, and Alexandra the very best of luck for what promises to be an incredible career ahead.'

Another thrilling engagement awaiting Alexandra was singing alongside the legendary Sir Elton John, who had arranged a huge concert at the O2 Arena to usher in the New Year. As he explained, as a teetotaller, working at New Year was a positive. He said, 'I do not drink any more. I've been sober for eighteen and a half years so New Year is always a predicament for me because we usually don't do anything.

'I've never really liked New Year's Eve... never enjoyed it that much. I'm a musician and would rather be playing.'

As *The X Factor* winner, Alexandra was invited to appear at the show. This was exciting for her but confusing for onlookers, given past statements Elton had made about *The X Factor* and other reality-television shows. Earlier in December, as Alexandra was crowned *X Factor* queen, Elton had launched a diatribe against the show while performing another gig at the O2. He told the audience at the time he would rather have his 'cock bitten off by an Alsatian than watch the show'. Meanwhile, in 2006 he had said, 'The X Factor is a cruise-ship show. I've got nothing against the people who go on – good luck to them. But I hate how they're treated. They're given an awful sense of stardom and pressure straight away but they're only successful until the next series. The record companies sell a lot of records and those people are gone. It's cruel. Will Young is the best thing that's ever come out of those shows. He has proved himself. But it's no way to find talent. I want to hear new songwriters, people who are creating their own stuff, not just singing my songs every week.'

Alexandra was definitely billed to appear and sing 'Hallelujah'. She was cheered hugely as she took the stage. She told her appreciative audience, 'Please join in with this song because I know you know the words. I just want to say thank you so much to everyone here tonight and enjoy your evening!'

Wearing a sleek back dress with her hair extra-straightened, she looked exceptionally good on the dry-ice-flooded O2 stage. Here she was back at the venue where she had auditioned six months earlier at the boot-camp stage. But now she was a confirmed star in her own right, as she demonstrated in the final rousing conclusion of her number-one hit. 'Thank you very much and Happy New Year to you all,' she said before leaving the stage.

She later wrote on her blog, 'For all those who

watched the Elton gig, thank you so much! I was so scared before I walked on that stage! It was amazing to be there at the O2, I've ALWAYS wanted to perform there!! And another special moment that night was when I met Elton himself! AHHHHH! He is such a lovely guy!! And I'm hoping one day that I can work with him! Fingers crossed!!'

Appearances in front of royalty and Sir Elton John and escorted visits to Harrods: all this was just what Alexandra had dreamed of. On winning *The X Factor* she had told Simon Cowell that she planned to work her socks off. And as we have seen, she was already slogging away prior to entering the show, albeit not in such glamorous surroundings. However, everyone deserves a holiday and so it was that she jetted off to Mauritius with her fellow *X Factor* contestant and new best friend Ruth Lorenzo. There the pair had a great holiday, soaking up the sun while Britain shivered. The media followed their every move, with a *Mirror* report stating, 'Alexandra Burke has swapped *The X Factor* for the Factor 10 on a holiday in Mauritius with her new best pal, fellow finalist Ruth Lorenzo. The pair already have the right gear for their A-list lifestyles... skimpy bikinis, floaty kaftans and oversized sunglasses. And in a dazzling red swimsuit, looks like Alex has done the showbiz weight loss thing too.' (She was photographed back home in London in February 2009 looking even slimmer.)

Meanwhile, the *Daily Mail* ran with the headline: HALLELUJAH, IT'S A HOLIDAY AT LAST FOR *X FACTOR* WINNER ALEXANDRA... AND FORMER RIVAL RUTH GOES TOO.

While holidaying, Alexandra was said to have got very friendly with a local lad called Maurice. Samoan-born Maurice works at Blues Diving Centre in the posh Belle Mare Plage hotel. A friend of Alex's said, 'Alex got back on Friday and said one of the best things about her break was meeting Maurice. She just wanted a bit of fun before focusing on her debut album.'

On her return, she made no mention of Maurice in her blog but did say she had a wonderful time. 'I went there with Ruth and my friend Adam, who is my make-up artist! We had a blast! But to be honest, by day seven I was itching to come home and start working! Lol! Mad I know!! But I'm so excited about 2009! I was there for nine days and I went to swim with dolphins, chilled out and had BBQ on the beach. Then I went around to loads of local places in Mauritius and it was amazing to see another culture! Since I've been back it's been non-stop lol. But I'm loving every minute of it!! At the moment I'm at City airport waiting to board the plane to go to Dublin. I hear it's cold out there and I only have my little jacket... I wish someone had told me sooner! Haha!'

On their return, Alexandra and Lorenzo went house hunting together. They soon found a luxury Riverside apartment with floor-to-wall windows offering breathtaking views of the Thames. A source said, 'Alex isn't ready to live by herself yet. She and Ruth have become firm friends in the past three months. Ruth's been an absolute rock.'

It sounds like a classy pad. However, during the preparations for *The X Factor* tour, reports suggested that Alexandra might not be earning the vast sums the public associate with stars of the music business. 'Having won *The X Factor*, sung a duet with Beyoncé and seen her debut single, "Hallelujah", become last year's biggest seller and the Christmas No1, you could be forgiven for thinking that Alexandra Burke has the world at her feet,' began a shock-horror-style story in the *Daily Mail*. 'Fame, fortune and a life of glittering stardom are clearly hers, with penthouse apartments, designer dresses and abundant wealth. If you believe all the talk of stardom, success and million-pound deals propagated by shows such as *The X Factor* and *Britain's Got Talent*, that is. Yet behind the glitz and the glamour lies a starker reality concerning the lives of these manufactured stars – one that should give any aspiring contestant pause for thought.

'Far from becoming an instant millionaire,

Alexandra Burke will have earned barely enough to afford a seat on Simon Cowell's private jet, let alone a jet of her own. And if you think she is set to rake in the big bucks in the near future, you may want to think again. For the upcoming *X Factor* tour – which sees Alexandra, along with the other finalists, perform a series of concerts around the country – she will earn only £250 for some performances, despite the fact that tickets for the 25 shows cost between £30 and £45 each. Venues such as the 20,000-seat O2 Arena in London are set to make more than £600,000 from ticket sales alone when the show rolls into town. And she is luckier than the other finalists, such as *The X Factor* runners-up, the four-piece boy band JLS, who will earn £100 each for some of the gigs.'

Tabby Callaghan – who finished third in the inaugural series of *The X Factor* – was quick to speak up in support of these claims. 'Anyone who thinks they are going on *The X Factor* to make big money will be in for a big shock,' says Callaghan. 'Contestants think it is the beginning of their career but there is nothing to back it up. They set you up for this big thing and then after the show you can't sign with anyone for three months. By then the heat has fizzled out and you're on your own. I got around £400 for each live gig. But I ended up losing money because I had to pay my expenses.'

However, Cowell denies the accuracy of some of the

reported figures. 'There is no pressure for anyone to go on to the tour if they don't want to,' he says. 'It is not slave labour. I won't go into precise figures because that is confidential but these people will earn around about £50,000 each on *The X Factor* tour. For any kid who wants to get into the music business and who hasn't got a recording contract... well, it is a good deal. To put them in front of 16 million television viewers over a period of time and then pay them £50,000 for three months' work? That is not a bad deal.'

Not a bad deal at all. But the post-show fortunes of *X Factor* winners have been mixed to say the least. The winner of the first series was Steve Brookstein. Before outlining the disaster that befell him after the show, it is worth mentioning that on the night of the final he received 5.5 million votes, which is 800,000 more than Alexandra received. Therefore, his story serves as a warning sign to her to not be complacent. In the immediate wake of the show, Brookstein had a number-one hit with his cover of 'Against All Odds' and then a number-one album of middle-of-the-road covers. But within three months, he lost his £1 million record deal and has since ended up singing on ferries, in pubs, at Butlins and in the touring version of the Madness-inspired musical *Our House*. The disagreement with the show came about because Brookstein wanted his second album to be full of songs he had written himself and Cowell refused. Undeterred, he released the album himself, entitling it *40,000 Things*. A *Sunday Mirror* columnist quipped that it was an apt title as there would be '40,000 things left in the Woolworth's bargain bin.'

'Simon Cowell put me into suits,' says Brookstein. 'He said, "We want you to look and dress and act like a star." I took that on board. It's all about personality – if you're marketable, if you're easy to work with. They don't want somebody who is going to have an opinion. And I'm branded as bitter. Well, no shit, Sherlock! It did take a long time to be philosophical, and not be angry about it.'

As he was one of the older contestants and, thanks in part also to his gravelly voice, Brookstein was marked down as 'one for the ladies'. However, he says, he was not marketed to take advantage of this, especially when compared to the treatment of the first series' runners-up. 'I was always branded the housewives' favourite – cheeky smile, romantic songs – so you would've thought that my album would come out on Mother's Day, the biggest-selling point of the year,' he rails. 'G4 [who finished second to him] released their album for Mother's Day and sold a quarter of a million records in a week. My album came out for Father's Day. Why? Thanks, guys.' This was clearly one of the straws that broke the camel's back when it came to relations between Brookstein and the record label.

Ironically, his career had actually been on an upwards trajectory immediately prior to *The X Factor*. Indeed, it could be argued that the show did not only fail to take him forwards, but actually took him backwards. 'I'd just supported Dionne Warwick at the Fairfield Halls,' he recalls wistfully, 'and I was asked to support Lionel Richie at Wembley. I never got to do it because I chose *The X Factor* instead. So I don't know whether things would've turned out better but I'm in a happy place. I may not have had the recognised success of other winners but, in terms of success as a human, I feel blessed that I've kept my integrity. I actually quite like *The X Factor*.'

It is worth restating that this set of disasters befell a man who received nearly a million *more* votes than Alexandra, and his experiences should serve as a warning to anyone attempting to make their name through *The X Factor*.

But the next winner, Shayne Ward, enjoyed far more positive experiences in the wake of his triumph. Here *The X Factor* got what they wanted – a successful artist who enjoyed a largely happy relationship with the record label after the show – and the winner got what he wanted too – fame and fortune. Having beaten soul singer Andy Abraham to win the second series, Ward seemed set for a successful career. He had a great voice and a fantastic pop image, with boyish good looks to match. After the competition, his mentor Louis Walsh became his manager under a joint venture with Global Publishing and Walsh Global Management, and Ward signed a contract with Sony BMG. His winner's single, 'That's My Goal', became the Christmas number one and stayed there for four weeks. Indeed, it stayed in the top 75 for a very respectable 21 weeks. It was then the fourth-fastest-selling UK single of all time, beaten only by Elton John's 'Candle in the Wind', Will Young's 'Anything Is Possible'/'Evergreen', and Gareth Gates's 'Unchained Melody', which sold 685,000, 403,000 and 335,000 copies in their first days of sale respectively. To date, it has sold over a million copies.

Having conquered the singles charts, it was time for him to record and release an album. The self-titled album was a number-one in eight countries and went platinum. His second album, *Breathless*, released in November 2007, a year on from his *X Factor* triumph, was ranked number two on the Channel 4 list of the 100 Best Albums of 2007 and was also one of the best-selling albums in 2007 in the UK, debuting at number two in the charts and once more going platinum. Ward undertook a successful tour to promote it, performing at a host of top venues including London's O2 Arena.

Then it seemed for a while that a natural disaster was going to wreck the momentum that Ward had built up. It was reported that he had developed vocal cord nodules, the condition that had wrecked the singing career of the legendary Julie Andrews. He was flown out to the East Coast of America for treatment. 'It was very serious indeed because it caused me so many major problems that I couldn't sing,' he recalls. 'I asked the doctor, Dr Cantor, who was the surgeon, and I said I needed him to be straight with me, "Is there a chance that it might not come back?" and he said it was straight down the line, "fifty/fifty you may not get your voice back". So he said, "What do you want to do?" and I had to follow it through to see whether it came back or not, and it's the best decision I ever made.'

He is back singing now and is – in contrast to Brookstein – extremely grateful to *The X Factor* for the career it has given him. 'I'm very proud to have come from *The X Factor*. I will never change saying that because it has put me in a place now where I absolutely love the position that I am in. I'm doing something that not many people do for a living, and I want to do this for a living so I'm very proud to have been from there.

'You do find real talent on the shows. A lot of people do put down these shows and say that they are not real talent but it would be great to see people who are actually in the music industry now whether they could actually do that, if they could stand in front of three of the most powerful people in pop, and in front of the million and see if they could do it. It does give some people the chance to get into the music industry.' He is now starting work on his third album and has returned to *The X Factor* studio to sing as a guest during the live shows.

The third series produced the legendary Leona Lewis. Although we have already heard of some of her achievements earlier in this book, it is well worth returning to her in order to demonstrate just how successful an *X Factor* winner can become. Her list of global achievements is as breathtakingly successful as it is long. Since winning the third series of *The X Factor*, Lewis has become nothing short of an international superstar. Her debut single, 'A Moment Like This', broke a world record after it was downloaded over 50,000 times within 30 minutes of its release. The follow-up single, 'Bleeding Love', was the biggest-selling single of 2008 in her home country and worldwide topped more than 30 international singles charts, including the United States, Canada, Australia, Japan, New Zealand, Mexico, the Republic of Ireland, France, Italy, Germany and Russia, and has since become the biggest-selling single of the 21st century by a female. By this time her fame was well and truly global.

Then came her first album, *Spirit*, which was the

fastest-selling debut album ever in the United Kingdom and Ireland. Released in the United States of America in 2008, *Spirit* went straight to number 1 on the United States' Billboard 200 album chart, making her the first British solo artist to top the chart with a debut album and an American superstar, thanks to Cowell's canny combination of contacts and know-how. Lewis's fifth UK single was a cover of Snow Patrol song 'Run', the fastest-selling digital-only release of all time, after it sold 69,244 in just two days. By the end of the first week of sales, download figures had reached 131,593, some 8,000 below the first-week sales of 'A Moment Like This'. Lewis reached number one in both Ireland and the UK purely from downloads of the song.

Her fame grows and grows. In 2009 she is due to release her second album, which is set to become another smash hit. Just prior to that release, she will publish her autobiography in which her route to fame and experiences after *The X Factor* will be laid bare. She also has a plan for a world tour in 2010 and wants to launch her own range of ethical fashion accessories. A vegetarian, Lewis turned down an offer for a promotional deal from Harrods owner Mohammed Al Fayed on the grounds that his store is the only one in the United Kingdom to still sell fur. She has also won numerous awards, including an Ivor Novello award for 'A Moment Like This', a Billboard

Year End award in the category of New Artist, a Virgin Media Music Award for 'Bleeding Love', a Capital Award as Favourite Female Music Artist. *Cosmopolitan* have named her their Newcomer of the Year and she has been nominated for five Brit Awards.

Whereas Brookstein had clashed with Cowell in the aftermath of his *X Factor* victory, Lewis says she and her guru have seen eye to eye. 'Simon mentors me and he's still like a mentor now so when I was doing the album he was always on the same page as me and he shared the same vision so it was very much a joint thing,' she says. She has visited Cowell in his flash Los Angeles home. 'It was like a James Bond house,' she says. 'We went up the drive and there was his Lamborghini – or some car that was very low to the ground – and his house was all glass. It was amazing. His mum and Terri [Seymour, Cowell's then-girlfriend] were there and I went over to listen to some songs. He's been very, very involved in the album. Obviously, he's so busy going between London and LA that I generally talk to him on the phone, but we usually agree on the songs. He always gives me feedback on what he likes and tells me to follow my instincts. We always had a really good relationship.'

Like Ward, she is proud of her *X Factor* connection. 'The show has given me this opportunity,' she affirms. 'Before going on *The X Factor* I'd always be in the studio and performing in shows whenever I could. I never try and dismiss it because at the end of the day it's given me the opportunity. All the support I got was lovely and I'm grateful to be in the position I am now.' She adds, 'I am nervous but there's no way I'm going to let this opportunity slide. Whatever happens to me from now on, I can't ever imagine wanting to distance myself from *The X Factor*, or having a bad word to say about it, because the show opened doors for me that had never opened before.'

Where Lewis's experience differed from all previous reality-show winners was that she did not release her album until a year after the show. This turned out to be a masterstroke, yet she admits she was worried at times as she disappeared from the public eye. 'I knew everyone was saying, "Where's Leona gone? She's just another reality-TV show singer who's disappeared," and it was worrying that some people were writing me off already. But it was necessary to take that time to make the album because we all wanted to get it right. I've always wanted to be a singer and, now that I've been given this opportunity, I want longevity in this industry. Taking time over the album was fundamental to my development as an artist.'

That development has paid dividends and Lewis is, to date, the most successful *X Factor* champion. Everyone connected to the show is enormously proud of their part in her success. Could they repeat or even surpass that feat in the fourth series?

The short answer is no. The long answer is the disappointing story that befell the fourth winner of *The X Factor*, Scot Leon Jackson. The young crooner was expected to come second on the evening of the final, behind the hugely talented Welsh tenor Rhydian. However, in something of a shock, Jackson won. Bookmakers Ladbrokes said it was 'the biggest shock in the history of reality-TV betting. He saved us from a bumper payout,' said spokesman Nick Weinberg. 'He'll definitely be top of our Christmas-card list.'

'I decided to pursue this because I loved singing,' Jackson told host O'Leary when his victory was confirmed. 'Then, as it went along, I knew I could potentially change my mum's life and I've just done it.'

In the aftermath of his victory, Jackson has enjoyed some successful moments but it has not been quite the life-changing experience he hoped for. He topped the charts with his winner's single 'When You Believe'. However, his follow-up only charted at number three. Then came his album, which has the unwelcome distinction of being the first by a winning *X Factor* act not to top the charts. It spent only one week in the top 10. He has since criticised *The X Factor*, saying, 'It gets clouded these days when the judges are having their confrontations. It should be more about the acts.' His experiences are far closer to those of

Brookstein's disaster than they are the successes enjoyed by Ward and Lewis. 'It still doesn't seem real,' said Jackson when he won. 'I've only sung karaoke in local pubs, and only since January of this year, because I turned 18 last December.'

Some fear that he will soon be back singing karaoke once again. True, it would have been hard for anyone to live up to the staggering success of Lewis, but Jackson's performance since the show is a bitter disappointment.

It is his legacy that Alexandra must overcome. In a sense, Jackson's limited success plays into her hands. Just as it was hard for him to live up to Lewis's example, so Alexandra will find it hard not to beat Jackson's. Given that she has often been compared with Leona Lewis, it seems most likely that her experiences in the aftermath of *The X Factor* will come closest to hers. Indeed, in the days following Alexandra's victory, Lewis sent a text message to a member of *The X Factor* team, asking them to pass on her congratulations and respect to the new winner. Given that Cowell was not even her mentor on the show, the two seemed to share an extraordinarily good rapport.

In fact, it was Cowell who seemed to help Alexandra across the finishing line. In the final three weeks of the competition, he was seen to withdraw some of his support for his own act – Eoghan Quigg – and transfer it to Alexandra. Given the usually partisan behaviour of *The X Factor* judges, this break with tradition suggests that Cowell did indeed see huge potential in Alexandra and wanted to help her to victory – and to be associated with that victory. That support was vital – as only became clear when *The X Factor* voting figures were revealed after the series had finished.

Interestingly, Alexandra had not been winning the show week in, week out. Often the winner is later revealed to have dominated the voting throughout the live shows. But in the case of *The X Factor* 2008, Alexandra was not the early frontrunner. Indeed, in week one of the competition she only came sixth, with 7.2 per cent of the vote compared to frontrunner Eoghan's 21.19 per cent share. The consistent leader was, in fact, Eoghan Quigg, who polled the most votes in the first five weeks. Then Diana Vickers won week six before Eoghan reclaimed the lead for a week. It was only then, in the final three weeks, that Alexandra took the lead and won comfortably, with Eoghan Quigg relegated to third place in the final. Cowell's vocal backing of her at the close clearly had an effect.

Perhaps another factor that helped Alexandra take the lead from Eoghan Quigg was the incessant speculation in the media that Quigg was having a relationship with fellow contestant Vickers. The pair were certainly very close as friends at least. But midway through the finals, speculation reached fever pitch that Vickers had left her boyfriend, student Chris Jones. 'Diana and Chris have split. She is overwhelmed with everything right now and says she doesn't want any boyfriend,' a source told the *Sun*. Week in, week out, the story seemed to change. First, they were behaving like a young couple in love, going on dates together, then they would laugh off the rumours. Then Cowell described them as 'two kids in love' at an *X Factor* press conference. Whatever the truth of the matter, the public got tired of the story and this might have led to voters being less inclined to support Quigg. Could it also be that, given that his appeal was thought to be largely among the 'granny voters', rumours of him romancing a girl who already had a boyfriend offended them? (The pair have since signed deals with the Epic record label, so they are together in that sense if nothing else.)

None of this is to detract from the fact that Alexandra was a thoroughly deserving winner in her own right. Her performances in the final three weeks of the competition were so good that it might well be as simple as that – she sang her way to victory. As a winner, she is certainly well positioned to emulate Lewis's achievements. There have even been suggestions attributed to the Cowell camp that she could do even better than Lewis. Time will tell.

But as it seemed to work so well last time, Alexandra will follow Lewis's lead in delaying the release of her debut album. At first it was planned for the album to be released as early as March 2009. Then bosses decided to delay it, as they had successfully done with Lewis. 'Syco were planning a quick release – possibly as early as March in time for Mothers' Day. But they have reconsidered and will now go for the autumn – probably November,' the source says. 'They want to wait to find the right songs and let her polish her skills, like they did with Leona. She can then launch it on a live *X Factor* show.'

Alongside her all the way will be Cheryl Cole, who has proved to be not just a mentor but also a friend to Alexandra. The Girls Aloud star's first series as an *X Factor* judge proved to be a massive success and she looks set to become a part of the show's furniture. And a popular one. 'Knowing what we now know about her upbringing and her strength of character, plus the fact she herself emerged from a talent show, well, of course everyone watches her,' said Jane Bruton, editor of *Grazia*, which named Cole fashion icon of the year in the wake of the series.

'Cheryl has made an enormous contribution to the show. Would we want her back? Oh, of course we would!' said Lorraine Heggessey, chief executive of Talkback Thames, the company behind the show.

A more route-one celebration of Cole's newfound national-treasure status came from the queen of journalism Julie Burchill. In an article comparing Lily Allen and Cole, she wrote, If I had to choose either Cheryl Cole or Lily Allen as my daughter, it would definitely be the former. Cheryl has come a long way from her youthful brawling in toilets and now shows every sign of growing into a dignified, level-headed and compassionate national treasure.'

Cole later wept with gratitude for Burchill's kind and supportive words.

As Alexandra explained, she and Cole remained close even after the show. 'I love her to pieces,' she told *Grazia* magazine. 'Our friendship... it got better and better as the weeks went by. She means the world to me, that woman. Even last night, I texted her. I wrote, "I know this sounds really weird and don't think I'm weird, Cheryl – but I miss you so much!" She texted me right back: "I've actually got withdrawal symptoms!"'

In the same interview, she denied reports that she had been told to lose weight during her *X Factor* journey, although lose weight she did, dropping two dress sizes during the live finals. Rumours then erupted that either Cowell or Walsh had ordered her to lose weight. Not true, she insists. 'No, no one did. Not at all. Though I am very happy with my weight now. I'm hoping to stay this size. Eight to ten. I feel better in myself. I've got addicted to healthy eating. I won't eat any carbs after eight in the evening. I'm not going to fill my belly up with pizzas. I remember, I used to eat Indian takeaway at eleven o'clock and then go straight to bed. Ridiculous.'

Cheryl Cole had provoked gasps for her super-thin physique during *The X Factor* finals but Alexandra had surprising news for *Grazia* readers. 'Well, the thing is Cheryl eats a lot! Serious! Oh, my God, that woman can eat like a horse. When I went round to her house and we had Domino's, I had two slices of pizza and she had about five. She's got one hell of a metabolism!'

As well as nights in with Cole, Alexandra was enjoying nights out too. She was snapped at the *Elle* magazine Style Awards, wearing a Dolce and Gabbana sequinned nautical outfit. While there, she reportedly gave *Little Britain* star David Walliams the brush-off. Walliams is said to have approached Alexandra and said, 'You're stunning – even prettier in real life. Do you have a boyfriend? Why don't you have a boyfriend? Can I be your boyfriend?'

Alexandra replied that she was concentrating on her career, but added that her mother was a 'huge fan' of Walliams.

He said, 'Well, if she looks like you, I'll take her number instead!'

Fame is a mixed bag for anyone to experience. Alongside the positive side there is always a price to pay, as Alexandra discovered in the tabloid obsession with her love life. Further negative headlines came when Alexandra's mother was accused of benefit fraud. Claims were made that Bell was getting paid for gigs while claiming benefits worth £17,344 a year. 'I simply couldn't believe it,' she said, firmly denying the report. 'But I rang the council and they have admitted I am under suspicion of benefit fraud. I'm absolutely outraged.' She said it was also being assumed that Alexandra was assisting her financially – not true, she said. 'They think Alex is supporting me. If she's giving me money, I have to declare it – but she hasn't. She's not allowed to live in my house because that would cancel my benefits, but she's not. Alex came here for Christmas but she doesn't actually live with me.

'It looks like I'm a fraud because Alex came and stayed with her sick mother over Christmas for a few days. The council can come and search me right now. Officials have looked online at all the places I have appeared at and have contacted them all. But any money I've received I've given to the Kidney Patient Association. I am very mindful of the rules. On Christmas Day I stepped in for Alex at a restaurant but I didn't get paid – I got a Christmas dinner. I also sang at my hospital for the patients, but I didn't get paid for that either. I'm really upset about all this and very alarmed.'

The previous month the *Sun*'s showbusiness editor, Gordon Smart, had warned Alexandra that she would have to face intrusive press, but predicted that she could deal with it. Speaking to *The Xtra Factor: The Winners' Story*, he said, 'There will come a point when she'll have to put up with a lot of speculation about her private life but I think she's definitely got the personality to cope with it. I think she's got a really bright future.'

A happier family press moment came in an interview with the local newspaper, the *Islington Gazette*. Her mother said, 'This is just a normal Islington girl from the Cally and look what she has achieved. Alexandra has eclipsed me by a thousand light years – she has already topped any success I had.' She continued, 'I never quite reached the pinnacle and never had a number one. But Alexandra is in a different stratosphere now. As a parent, I can live the dream through her. My only concern is not seeing her so much – but she is a sensible girl and won't do anything silly.'

Alexandra's brother David, 21, an accountancy student, said, 'Seeing Alex on stage with Beyoncé brought home how much she has achieved and how far she has come. That old phrase "never give up" was proved on Saturday. It shows what anyone can achieve if they believe in themselves. When Dermot O'Leary said she had won I was crying tears of joy.' He added, 'I just want to thank the *Gazette* so much for its support. It's been unbelievable. When we saw the posters everywhere saying MAKE IT THE ALEX FACTOR it really touched us.'

Also involved in the local-newspaper interview was Alexandra's aunt Angela Gondzioulis, who flew from her home in Sydney, Australia to see the final. She said, 'I thought, I can't miss this, it's such an important event in Alexandra's life. I couldn't believe it was the same little girl who would dance in front of us!'

Brother David added, 'At the start of all of this Alexandra said she wanted Leona Lewis's luck to travel down the 38 bus route from Hackney to Islington. It looks like it has arrived.'

Local people were very proud of Alexandra's success. Their pride increased when Alexandra took part in a local initiative to raise money for a cervical-cancer charity. Dozens of people donated clothes to take part in the first celebrity clothes-swapping event that saw Islington residents who donated items receive points which could be exchanged for clothes donated by bona fide celebrities, and the famous faces were no Z-listers. They included singer Gwen Stefani, socialite Tara Palmer-Tomkinson, former *Blue Peter* presenter Konnie Huq, and Mel B and Mel C of the

Spice Girls. Money raised went to cervical-cancer charities Jo's Trust and Cervical Cancer Awareness Week. Also donating clothes was 1980s singer Sinitta, who used to date *X Factor*'s Simon Cowell. She said, 'I am so pleased to be helping this wonderful cause. Cervical cancer is such a killer in young women. And what better way to raise awareness than via shopping?'

Another famous face involved was Destiny's Child singer Kelly Rowland. She said, 'When I heard what they were doing I just had to be involved. I have donated a bracelet I wore for an event to show my support.'

Alexandra was honoured that her fame put her alongside such figures and gave her the opportunity to donate to a great cause. Another way she used her fame for a good cause was via an imaginative initiative set up by a breast-cancer charity. The charity donated, on a year-by-year basis, a pink Mini to Alexandra. 'And if I'm papped in it,' she explains, 'the money goes to breast-cancer research. Let's get it papped! Good, eh?' Here the true beauty of Alexandra's character emerged: she was delighted by the chance to use her growing fame for a wonderful cause.

Meanwhile, her ambition for her career knows no boundaries. Having watched the success of UK acts at the 2009 Grammys, she is keen to crack America, as her *X Factor* predecessor Leona Lewis did. 'Watching

Coldplay take away three Grammys was just amazing to watch – it inspired me so much. I am so happy for them. For that to happen to me… wow, that would be incredible. I'm still recovering from Christmas but I still have to pinch myself and realise it's happening – then before I know it I am nominated for a Brit Award, which is out of this world. These things all happens so fast and anything is possible now. I want that.'

Soon after making this ambition public, Alexandra's American dream began to come true with the news that she had signed a £3 million record deal in the States with the mighty Epic label. The five-album deal hooked her up with the same team that made Rihanna and Beyoncé so huge. 'Epic think that Alexandra can follow in Leona's footsteps,' a music industry source explained in the *Sun*. 'The US market loves women with big voices – and Alex certainly has that. If she comes close to Leona's success, it will be a job well done.'

Despite only being famous for a matter of months and having the States only in her sights at this stage, Alexandra came in for criticism from an American singer, Lady GaGa, who knocked *The X Factor* winner off the number-one spot in the singles chart in January 2009. Lady GaGa said, 'If you win a TV show and you have a hit record, you sort of have a false understanding of what it means to earn success.

The shows are set up for a winner, for someone to win. Whereas with someone like me, who writes my own songs, you have to set yourself up to win.'

They were sour words from GaGa, who was proving to be a bad winner, having got the number-one spot. Alexandra shouldn't worry though, as soon after this outburst she was told that she had been nominated for a Brit Award for 'Hallelujah' in the Best Single category. And although she didn't win, she can't have been too unhappy to lose out to her friend and mentor Cheryl Cole's band, who took the award for their single 'The Promise'.

Extraordinary promise surrounded Alexandra as she spent 2009 out of the public eye, preparing for her debut album launch in the autumn. This was a tactic that Cowell and his team first tried – to such stunning effect – with Leona Lewis, whose phenomenal global success and star quality make a mockery of the cynicism of reality television's critics, as does that of Cole's Girls Aloud and so many others. During the summer, the stylish Alexandra signed a major deal with Dolce & Gabbana as one of the faces of D&G's younger clothes collection. It was even rumoured that Domenico Dolce and Stefano Gabbana were personally behind the decision to sign her up. With such lucrative deals coming her way, Alexandra was set to emulate Lewis, whose personal fortune runs into millions of pounds.

Naturally, public anticipation for the album was

high. Demos of potential tracks were leaked onto the internet in the summer of 2009, much to the annoyance of her label and management. Yet – whether or not they went on to form part of her album – they pointed to a cracking debut from the *X Factor* champion. Alexandra worked extremely hard on the material, often sitting up late into the evening with top songwriters crafting lyrics for some of the tracks. 'Things have been very hectic, working very, very hard!' she wrote on her official website. 'But [I'm] having so much fun at the same time. I cannot wait to share my music with you all. We have nearly chosen what the first single is going to be and I'm extremely happy with it.'

Much of the work on the album took place in Los Angeles. Though Alexandra often felt homesick, she spoke with typical enthusiasm about life in the glitzy Californian city. 'It's so lovely here, the weather is a bit up and down but it's still beautiful,' she said. 'I'm having a blast! I've been going out to dinner here any chance I can and the places here to eat are unreal! The food is amazing. I've met Jay Z, Timberland and I saw Beyoncé again, but this time I didn't cry! She is so beautiful and once again welcomed me with open arms. I'm living a dream!' A dream, indeed – and one she was keen to share. She flew family members out to Los Angeles and let them enjoy a part of her glamorous new life.

Travelling round different parts of America, the girl from Islington loved New York but decided that San Francisco was the 'perfect' city for her. When she returned to England the north Londoner was happy to be in more familiar surroundings and even spontaneously burst into applause as her plane landed. With widespread hopes that she will emulate or even better the colossal international success of Lewis, Alexandra will no doubt spend plenty more time flying around the world. One hopes – and suspects – she will keep her feet on the ground whatever is about to come her way.

Alexandra is a winner. Not just in terms of The X Factor, but in life in general. She fought her way to the top and every bit of success that comes her way is richly deserved and earned. She sets a marvellous example to the youth of Britain, showing them that they can get where they deserve to be, provided they are prepared to combine hard work with determination. In fact, she sets a marvellous example to us all, regardless of age. For all who dream – and who doesn't? – we can watch her making it big and conquering her career of choice and know that we too can make our dreams come true. Who could not be moved and inspired by her tearful determination to win X Factor and that look of sheer joy and shock on her face when she did win.

To see her living her dream is enough to push any

observers close to tears themselves. Rarely can a reality show victory be more deserved. 'What life's thrown at me is quite tricky, but I'm glad as it's allowed me to have thick skin,' she says. 'I've struggled – we all go through it – but it's taught me a lot.' Then her eyes light up and she breaks into a smile and adds, 'I have to pinch myself every day. I always have to give thanks to the universe. None of this was happening six months ago. The support has been phenomenal. It's weird how my life has turned around. I'm a happier person. The *X Factor* has turned my life around.'

You can't say fairer than that, can you? Long may she reign.

ACKNOWLEDGEMENTS

Thanks to Chris Morris, Lucian Randall, John Blake, Rosie Ries and Mary Tobin.